AWARENESS

AWARENESS

The Key to Living in Balance

osho

·

insights for a
new way of living

St. Martin's Griffin ♒ New York

www.stmartins.com

Editing and compilation by Sarito Carol Neiman

ISBN 0-312-27563-3

10   9

Contents

Contents

Foreword

One of the most important things to be understood about man is that man is asleep. Even while he thinks he is awake, he is not. His wakefulness is very fragile; his wakefulness is so tiny it doesn't matter at all. His wakefulness is only a beautiful name but utterly empty.

You sleep in the night, you sleep in the day—from birth to death you go on changing your patterns of sleep, but you never really awaken. Just by opening the eyes don't befool yourself that you are awake. Unless the inner eyes open—unless your inside becomes full of light, unless you can see yourself, who you are—don't think that you are awake. That is the greatest illusion man lives in. And once you accept that you are already awake, then there is no question of making any effort to be awake.

The first thing to sink deep in your heart is that you are asleep, utterly asleep. You are dreaming, day in, day out. You are dreaming sometimes with open eyes and sometimes with closed eyes, but you are dreaming—you *are* a dream. You are not yet a reality.

Of course in a dream whatsoever you do is meaningless. Whatsoever you think is pointless, whatsoever you project remains part of your dreams and never allows you to see that which is. Hence all the buddhas have insisted on only one thing: Awaken! Continuously, for centuries, their whole teaching can be contained in a single phrase: Be awake. And they have been devising methods, strategies; they have been creating contexts and spaces and energy fields in which you can be shocked into awareness.

> ⌁
>
> The first thing to sink deep in your heart is that you are asleep, utterly asleep. You are dreaming, day in, day out. You are dreaming sometimes with open eyes and sometimes with closed eyes, but you are dreaming— you *are* a dream. You are not yet a reality.

Yes, unless you are shocked, shaken to your very foundations, you will not awaken. The sleep has been so long that it has reached to the very core of your being; you are soaked in it. Each cell of your body and each fiber of your mind has become full of sleep. It is not a small phenomenon. Hence great effort is needed to be alert, to be attentive, to be watchful, to become a witness.

If all the buddhas of the world agree on any one single theme, this is it—that man as he is, is asleep, and man as he should be, should be awake. Wakefulness is the goal and wakefulness is the taste of all their teachings. Zarathustra, Lao Tzu, Jesus, Buddha, Bahauddin, Kabir, Nanak—all the awakened ones have been teaching one single theme . . . in different languages, in different metaphors, but their song is the same. Just as the sea tastes of salt— whether the sea is tasted from the north or from the east or from the west, the sea always tastes of salt—the taste of buddhahood is wakefulness.

But you will not make any effort if you go on believing that you are already awake. Then there is no question of making any effort—why bother?

And you have created religions, gods, prayers, rituals, out of your dreams—your gods are as much part of your dreams as anything else. Your politics is part of your dreams, your religions are part of your dreams, your poetry, your painting, your art—whatsoever you do, because you are asleep, you do things according to your own state of mind.

Your gods cannot be different from you. Who will create them? Who will give them shape and color and form? You create them, you sculpt them; they have eyes like you, noses like you—and minds like you! The Old Testament God says, "I am a very jealous God!" Now who has created this God who is jealous? God cannot be jealous, and if God *is* jealous, then what is wrong in being jealous? If even God is jealous, why should you be thought to be doing something wrong when you are jealous? Jealousy is divine!

The Old Testament God says, "I am a very angry God! If you don't follow my commandments, I will destroy you. You will be thrown into hellfire for eternity. And because I am very jealous, don't worship anybody else. I cannot tolerate it." Who created such a God? It must be out of our own jealousy, out of our own anger, that you have created this image. It is your projection, it is your shadow. It echoes you and nobody else. And the same is the case with all gods of all religions.

It is because of this that Buddha never talked about God. He said, "What is the point of talking about God to people who are asleep? They will listen in their sleep. They will dream about whatsoever is said to them, and they will create their own gods—which will be utterly false, utterly impotent, utterly meaningless. It is better not to have such gods."

That's why Buddha is not interested in talking about gods. His whole interest is in waking you up.

It is said about a Buddhist enlightened master who was sitting by the side of the river one evening, enjoying the sound of the water, the sound of the wind passing through the trees . . . A man came and asked him, "Can you tell me in a single word the essence of your religion?"

The master remained silent, utterly silent, as if he had not heard the question. The questioner said, "Are you deaf or something?"

The master said, "I have heard your question, and I have answered it too! Silence is the answer. I remained silent—that pause, that interval, was my answer."

The man said, "I cannot understand such a mysterious answer. Can't you be a little more clear?"

So the master wrote on the sand "meditation," in small letters with his finger. The man said, "I can read now. It is a little better than at first. At least I have got a word to ponder over. But can't you make it a little more clear?"

The master wrote again "MEDITATION." Of course this time he wrote in bigger letters. The man was feeling a little embarrassed, puzzled, offended, angry. He said, "Again you write *meditation*? Can't you be a little clear for me?"

And the master wrote in big letters, capital letters, "M E D I - T A T I O N."

The man said, "You seem to be mad!"

The master said, "I have already come down very much. The first answer was the right answer, the second was not so right, the third even more wrong, the fourth has gone very wrong"—because when you write MEDITATION with capital letters you have made a god out of it.

That's why the word *God* is written with a capital G. Whenever you want to make something supreme, ultimate, you write it with a capital letter. The master said, "I have already committed a sin." He erased all those words he had written and he said, "Please listen to my first answer—only then I am true."

Silence is the space in which one awakens, and the noisy mind is the space in which one remains asleep. If

> Silence is the space in which one awakens, and the noisy mind is the space in which one remains asleep. If your mind continues chattering, you are asleep.

your mind continues chattering, you are asleep. Sitting silently, if the mind disappears and you can hear the chattering birds and no mind inside, a silence . . . this whistle of the bird, the chirping, and no mind functioning in your head, utter silence . . . then awareness wells up in you. It does not come from the outside, it arises in you, it grows in you. Otherwise, remember: you are asleep.

THE UNDERSTANDING

I never use the word renunciation *at all. I say: Rejoice in life, in love, in meditation, in the beauties of the world, in the ecstasy of existence—rejoice in everything! Transform the mundane into the sacred. Transform this shore into the other shore, transform the earth into paradise.*

And then indirectly a certain renunciation starts happening. But that happens, you don't do it. It is not a doing, it is a happening. You start renouncing your foolishnesses; you start renouncing rubbish. You start renouncing meaningless relationships. You start renouncing jobs that were not fulfilling to your being. You start renouncing places where growth was not possible. But I don't call it renunciation, I call it understanding, awareness.

If you are carrying stones in your hand thinking that they are diamonds, I will not tell you to renounce those stones. I will simply say, "Be alert and have another look!" If you yourself see that they are not diamonds, is there any need to renounce them? They will fall from your hands of their own accord. In fact, if you still want to carry them, you will have to make a great effort, you will have to bring great will, to still carry them. But you cannot carry them for long; once you have seen that they are useless, meaningless, you are bound to throw them away.

And once your hands are empty, you can search for the real treasures. And the real treasures are not in the future. The real treasures are right now, here.

OF MEN AND RATS

Wakefulness is the way to life.
The fool sleeps as if he were already dead,
but the master is awake and he lives forever.
He watches. He is clear.
How happy he is! For he sees that wakefulness is life.
How happy he is, following the path of the awakened.
With great perseverance he meditates, seeking freedom and
    happiness.

—from the *Dhammapada* of Gautama the Buddha

We go on living absolutely inattentive to what is happening around us. Yes, we have become very efficient in doing things. What we are doing, we have become so efficient in doing that we don't need any awareness to do it. It has become mechanical, automatic. We function like robots. We are not men yet; we are machines.

That's what George Gurdjieff used to say again and again, that man as he exists is a machine. He offended many people, because nobody likes to be called a machine. Machines like to be called gods; then they feel very happy, puffed up. Gurdjieff used to call people machines, and he was right. If you watch yourself, you will know how mechanically you behave.

The Russian physiologist Pavlov, and the American psychologist Skinner, are 99.9 percent right about man: they believe that man is a beautiful machine, that's all. There is no soul in him. I say 99.9 percent they are right; they only miss by a small margin. In that small margin are the buddhas, the awakened ones. But they can be forgiven, because Pavlov never came across a buddha—he came across millions of people like you.

Skinner has been studying men and rats and finds no difference. Rats are simple beings, that's all; man is a little more complicated.

Man is a highly sophisticated machine, rats are simple machines. It is easier to study rats; that's why psychologists go on studying rats. They study rats and they conclude about man—and their conclusions are almost right. I say "almost," mind you, because that one-tenth of one percent is the most important phenomenon that has happened. A Buddha, a Jesus, a Mohammed—these few awakened people are the real men. But where can B. F. Skinner find a buddha? Certainly not in America. . . .

I have heard:

A man asked a rabbi, "Why didn't Jesus choose to be born in twentieth-century America?"

The rabbi shrugged his shoulders and said, "In America? It would have been impossible. Where can you find a virgin, firstly? And secondly, where will you find three wise men?"

> Man is a highly sophisticated machine, rats are simple machines. It is easier to study rats, that's why psychologists go on studying rats. They study rats and they conclude about man—and their conclusions are almost right.

Where is B. F. Skinner going to find a buddha? And even if he can find a buddha, his preconceived prejudices, ideas, will not allow him to see. He will go on seeing his rats. He cannot understand anything that rats cannot do. Now, rats don't meditate, rats don't become enlightened. And he conceives of man only as a magnified form of a rat. And still I say that he is right about the greater majority of people; his conclusions are not wrong, and buddhas will agree with him about the so-called normal humanity. The normal humanity is utterly asleep. Even animals are not so asleep.

Have you seen a deer in the forest—how alert he looks, how watchfully he walks? Have you seen a bird sitting on the tree—how intelligently he goes on watching what is happening all around? You move toward the bird—there is a certain space he allows. Beyond that, one step more, and he flies away. He has a certain alertness about his territory. If somebody enters into that territory, then it is dangerous.

If you look around, you will be surprised: man seems to be the most asleep animal on the earth.

A woman buys a parrot at an auction of the furnishings of a fancy whorehouse and keeps the parrot's cage covered for two weeks, hoping to make it forget its profane vocabulary. When the cage is finally uncovered, the parrot looks around and remarks, *"Awrrk!* New house. New madam." When the woman's daughters come in, he adds, *"Awrrk!* New girls."

When her husband comes home that night, the parrot says, *"Awrrk! Awrrk!* Same old customers!"

Man is in a fallen state. In fact, that is the meaning of the Christian parable of the fall of Adam, his expulsion. Why were Adam and Eve expelled from paradise? They were expelled because they had eaten the fruit of knowledge. They were expelled because they had become *minds,* and they had lost their *consciousness.* If you become a mind, you lose consciousness—mind means sleep, mind means noise, mind means mechanicalness. If you become a mind, you lose consciousness.

Hence, the whole work that has to be done is to become consciousness again and lose the mind. You have to throw out of your system all that you have gathered as knowledge. It is knowledge that keeps you asleep; hence, the more knowledgeable a person is, the more asleep.

That has been my own observation too. Innocent villagers are far more alert and awake than the professors in the universities and the pundits in the temples. The pundits are nothing but parrots; the academicians in the universities are full of nothing but holy cow dung, full of absolutely meaningless noise—just minds and no consciousness.

People who work with nature—farmers, gardeners, woodcutters, carpenters, painters—they are far more alert than the people who function in the universities as deans and vice-chancellors and chancellors. Because when you work with nature, nature is alert. Trees are alert; their form of alertness is certainly different, but they are very alert.

Now there are scientific proofs of their alertness. If the woodcutter comes with an ax in his hand and with the deliberate desire to cut the tree, all the trees that see him coming tremble. Now there are scientific proofs about it; I am not talking poetry, I am talking science when I say this. Now there are instruments to measure whether the tree is happy or unhappy, afraid or unafraid, sad or ecstatic. When the woodcutter comes, all the trees that see him start trembling. They become aware that death is close by. And the woodcutter has not cut any tree yet—just his coming. . . .

And one thing more, far more strange—if the woodcutter is simply passing by, with no deliberate idea to cut a tree, then no tree becomes afraid. It is the same woodcutter, with the same ax. It seems that his *intention* to cut a tree affects the trees. It means that his intention is being understood; it means the very vibe is being decoded by the trees.

And one more significant fact has been observed scientifically: if

> Why were Adam and Eve expelled from paradise? They were expelled because they had eaten the fruit of knowledge. They were expelled because they had become *minds,* and they had lost their *consciousness.*

you go into the forest and kill an animal, not only the animal kingdom around becomes shaken, but trees also. If you kill a deer, all the
deer that are around feel the vibe of murder, become sad; a great
trembling arises in them. Suddenly they are afraid for no particular
reason at all. They may not have seen the deer being killed, but
somehow, in a subtle way, they are affected—instinctively, intuitively.
But it is not only the deer that are affected—the trees are affected,
the parrots are affected, the tigers are affected, the eagles are affected,
the grass leaves are affected. Murder has happened, destruction has
happened, death has happened—everything that is around is affected.
Man seems to be the most asleep. . . .

The sutras of Buddha have to be meditated on deeply, imbibed,
followed. He says:

Wakefulness is the way to life.

You are alive only in the proportion that you are aware. Awareness is the difference between death and life. You are not alive just
because you are breathing, you are not alive just because your heart
is beating. Physiologically you can be kept alive in a hospital, without
any consciousness. Your heart will go on beating and you will be
able to breathe. You can be kept in such a mechanical arrangement
that you will remain alive for years—in the sense of breathing and
the heart beating and the blood circulating. There are now many
people around the world in advanced countries who are just vegetating in the hospitals, because advanced technology has made it possible for your death to be postponed indefinitely—for years you can
be kept alive. If this is life, then you can be kept alive. But this is
not life at all. Just to vegetate is not life.

Buddhas have a different definition. Their definition consists of
awareness. They don't say you are alive because you can breathe,
they don't say you are alive because your blood circulates; they say
you are alive if you are awake. So except for the awakened ones,
nobody is really alive. You are corpses—walking, talking, doing
things—you are robots.

Wakefulness is the way to life, says Buddha. Become more wakeful and you will become more alive. <u>And life is God—there is no other God</u>. Hence Buddha talks about life and awareness. Life is the goal and awareness is the methodology, the technique to attain it.

The fool sleeps. . . .

And all are asleep, so all are foolish. Don't feel offended. The facts have to be stated as they are. You function in sleep; that's why you go on stumbling, <u>you go on doing things</u> you don't want to do. You go on doing things you have decided not to do. You go on doing things you know are not right to do, <u>and you don't do things that you know are right</u>.

How is this possible? Why can't you walk straight? Why do you go on getting trapped into bypaths? Why do you go on going astray?

A young man with a fine voice is asked to take part in a pageant play, though he tries to beg off, saying he always gets embarrassed under such circumstances. He is assured it will be very simple, and he will have only one line to say: "I come to snatch a kiss, and dart into the fray. Hark! I hear a pistol shot"—and then stride offstage.

At the performance he comes onstage, embarrassed already by the tight-fitting colonial knee breeches he has been made to put on at the last moment, and becomes completely unstrung at the sight of the beautiful heroine lying back on a garden seat awaiting him, in a white gown. He clears his throat and announces, "I come to kiss your snatch—no!—snatch a kiss, and fart into the dray—I mean, dart into the fray! Hark!—I hear a shistol pot—no!—a shostil pit, a pistil shit. Oh, batshit, ratshit, shit on you all! I never wanted to be in this damned play in the first place!"

This is what is happening. <u>Watch your life—everything that you go on doing is so confused and so confusing</u>. You don't have any clarity, you don't have any perceptiveness. You are not alert. You can't see, you can't hear—certainly you have ears so you can hear, but there is nobody inside to understand it. Certainly you have eyes so you can see, but there is nobody present inside. So your eyes go on seeing and your ears go on listening, but nothing is understood. And on each step you stumble, on each step you commit something wrong. And still you go on believing that you are aware.

Drop that idea completely. Dropping it is a great leap, a great step, because once you drop the idea that "I am aware," you will start seeking and searching for ways and means to be aware. So the first thing to sink into you is that you are asleep, utterly asleep.

Modern psychology has discovered a few things that are significant; although they have been discovered only intellectually, still it is a good beginning. If intellectually they have been discovered, then sooner or later they will also be experienced existentially.

Freud is a great pioneer; of course, not a buddha, but still a man of great significance because he was the first to make the idea accepted by the larger part of humanity that man has a great unconscious hidden in him. The conscious mind is only one-tenth, and the unconscious mind is nine times bigger than the conscious.

Then his disciple Jung went a little further, a little deeper, and discovered the collective unconscious. Behind the individual unconscious there is a collective unconscious. Now somebody is needed to discover one thing more, which is there, and I hope that sooner or later the psychological investigations that are going on will discover it—the cosmic unconscious. Buddhas have talked about it.

So we can talk about the conscious mind—a very fragile thing, a very small part of your being. Behind the conscious is the subconscious mind—vague, you can hear its whispering but you cannot figure it out. It is always there behind the conscious, pulling its strings. Third is the unconscious mind, which you come across only in dreams or when you take drugs. Then, the collective unconscious mind. You come across it only when you go into a deep inquiry into your unconscious mind; then you come across the collective unconscious. And if you go still further, deeper, you will come to the cosmic unconscious. The cosmic unconscious is nature. The collective unconscious is the whole of humanity that has lived up to now; it is part of you. The unconscious is your individual unconscious that society has repressed in you, that has not been allowed expression. Hence it comes by the back door in the night, in your dreams.

And the conscious mind . . . I will call it the so-called conscious mind because it is only so-called. It is so tiny, just a flicker, but even if it is just a flicker, it is important because it has the seed; the seeds are always small. It has great potential. Now a totally new dimension is opening up. Just as Freud opened the dimension below the conscious, Sri Aurobindo opened the dimension above the conscious. Freud and Sri Aurobindo are the two most important people of this age. Both are intellectuals, neither of them is an awakened person, but both have done a great service to humanity. Intellectually they have made us aware that we are not so small as we appear from the surface, that the surface is hiding great depths and heights.

Freud went into the depths, Sri Aurobindo tried to penetrate into the heights. Above our so-called conscious mind is the real conscious mind; that is attained only through meditation. When your ordinary conscious mind is added to meditation, when the ordinary conscious mind is plus meditation, it becomes the real conscious mind.

Beyond the real conscious mind is the superconscious mind. When you are meditating, you have only glimpses. Meditation is a groping in the dark. Yes, a few windows open up, but you fall back again and again. Superconscious mind means *samadhi*—you have attained a crystal-clear perceptiveness, you have attained an integrated awareness. Now you cannot fall below it; it is yours. Even in sleep it will remain with you.

Beyond the superconscious is the collective superconscious; the collective superconscious is what is known as "god" in the religions. And beyond the collective superconscious is the cosmic superconscious, which even goes beyond the gods. Buddha calls it *nirvana,* Mahavira calls it *kaivalya,* Hindu mystics have called it *moksha;* you can call it the truth.

> ❧
>
> You are just living in a small corner of your being—the tiny conscious mind. It is as if somebody has a palace and has completely forgotten about the palace and has started living on the porch—and thinks this is all.

These are the nine states of your being. And you are just living in a small corner of your being—the tiny conscious mind. It is as if somebody has a palace and has completely forgotten about the palace and has started living on the porch—and thinks this is all.

Freud and Sri Aurobindo are both great intellectual giants, pioneers, philosophers, but both are doing great guesswork. Instead of teaching students the philosophy of Bertrand Russell, Alfred North Whitehead, Martin Heidegger, Jean-Paul Sartre, it would be far better if people were taught more about Sri Aurobindo, because he is the greatest philosopher of this age. But he is completely neglected, ignored by the academic world. The reason is, even to read Sri Aurobindo will make you feel that you are unaware. And he himself is not a buddha yet, but still he will create embarrassment for you. If he is right, then what are you doing? Then why are you not exploring the heights of your being?

Freud was accepted with great resistance, but finally he was accepted. Sri Aurobindo is not even accepted yet. In fact there is not even any opposition to him; he is simply ignored. And the reason is clear. Freud talks about something below you—that is not so embarrassing; you can feel good knowing that you are conscious, and below your consciousness there is subconsciousness and unconsciousness and collective unconsciousness. But those states are all below you; you are at the top, you can feel very good. But if you study Sri Aurobindo, you will feel embarrassed, offended, because there are higher states than you—and man's ego never wants to accept that there is anything higher than him. Man wants to believe that he is the pinnacle, the climax, the Gourishankar, the Everest—that there is nothing higher than him. . . .

And it feels good—denying your own kingdom, denying your own heights, you feel very good. Look at the foolishness of it.

Buddha is right. He says: *The fool sleeps as if he were already dead, but the master is awake and he lives forever.*

Awareness is eternal, it knows no death. Only unawareness dies. So if you remain unconscious, asleep, you will have to die again. If you want to get rid of this whole misery of being born and dying again and again, if you want to get rid of the wheel of birth and death, you will have to become absolutely alert. You will have to reach higher and higher into consciousness.

And these things are not to be accepted on intellectual grounds; these things have to become experiential, these things have to become existential. I am not telling you to be convinced philosophically, because philosophical conviction brings nothing, no harvest. The real harvest comes only when you make great effort to wake yourself up.

But these intellectual maps can create a desire, a longing in you; can make you aware of the potential, of the possible; can make you aware that you are not what you appear to be—you are far more.

The fool sleeps as if he were already dead, but the master is awake and he lives forever.

He watches. He is clear.

Simple and beautiful statements. Truth is always simple and always beautiful. Just to see the simplicity of these two statements . . . but how much they contain. Worlds within worlds, infinite worlds— *He watches. He is clear.*

The only thing that has to be learned is watchfulness. Watch! Watch every act that you do. Watch every thought that passes in your mind. Watch every desire that takes possession of you. Watch even small gestures—walking, talking, eating, taking a bath. Go on watching everything. Let everything become an opportunity to watch.

Don't eat mechanically, don't just go on stuffing yourself—be very watchful. Chew well and watchfully . . . and you will be surprised how much you have been missing up to now, because each bite will give you tremendous satisfaction. If you eat watchfully, food will become more tasty. Even ordinary food tastes good if you are watchful; and if you are not watchful, you can eat the most tasty food but there will be no taste in it because there is nobody to watch. You simply go on stuffing yourself. Eat slowly, watchfully; each bite has to be chewed, tasted.

Smell, touch, feel the breeze and the sun rays. Look at the moon and become just a silent pool of watchfulness, and the moon will be reflected in you with tremendous beauty.

Move in life remaining continuously watchful. Again and again you will forget. Don't become miserable because of that; it is natural. For millions of lives you have never tried watchfulness, so it is simple, natural, that you go on forgetting again and again. But the moment you remember, again watch.

Remember one thing: when you remember that you have forgotten watching, don't become sorry, don't repent; otherwise, again you are wasting time. Don't feel miserable: "I missed again." Don't start feeling "I am a sinner." Don't start condemning yourself, because this is a sheer waste of time. Never repent for the past! Live in the moment. If you had forgotten, so what? It was natural—it has become a habit, and habits die hard. And these are not habits imbibed in one life; these are habits imbibed in millions of lives. So if you can remain watchful even for a few moments, feel thankful. Even those few moments are more than can be expected.

He watches. He is clear.

And when you watch, a clarity arises. Why does clarity arise out of watchfulness? Because the more watchful you become the more all your hastiness slows down. You become more graceful. As you watch, your chattering mind chatters less, because the energy that was becoming chattering is turning and becoming watchfulness—it is the same energy! Now more and more energy will be transformed into watchfulness, and the mind will not get its nourishment. Thoughts will start becoming thinner, they will start losing weight. Slowly, slowly, they will start dying. And as thoughts start dying, clarity arises. Now your mind becomes a mirror.

How happy he is! And when one is clear, one is blissful. Confusion is the root cause of misery; it is clarity that is the foundation of blissfulness. *How happy he is! For he sees that wakefulness is life.*

And now he knows there is no death, because wakefulness can never be destroyed. When death comes, you will watch it too. You will die watching—watching will not die. Your body will disappear, dust unto dust, but your watchfulness will remain; it will become part of the cosmic whole. It will become cosmic consciousness.

> ❧
> The more watchful you become the more all your hastiness slows down. You become more graceful. As you watch, your chattering mind chatters less, because the energy that was becoming chattering is turning and becoming watchfulness—it is the same energy!

In these moments the seers of the Upanishads declare, *"Aham brahmasmi—* I am the cosmic consciousness."* It is in such spaces that al-Hillaj Mansoor announced, *"Ana'l haq!—I am the truth!"* These are the heights, which are your birthright. If you are not getting them, only you are responsible and nobody else.

How happy he is! For he sees that wakefulness is life.

How happy he is, following the path of the awakened.

With great perseverance he meditates, seeking freedom and happiness.

Listen to these words attentively. *With great perseverance* . . . Unless you bring total effort to waking yourself up, it is not going to happen. Partial efforts are futile. You cannot be just so-so, you cannot be just

> ❧
>
> You cannot be just so-so, you cannot be just lukewarm. It is not going to help. Lukewarm water cannot evaporate, and lukewarm efforts to be alert are bound to fail. Transformation happens only when you put your total energy into it.

lukewarm. It is not going to help. Lukewarm water cannot evaporate, and lukewarm efforts to be alert are bound to fail.

Transformation happens only when you put your total energy into it. When you are boiling at a hundred degrees centigrade, then you evaporate, then the alchemical change happens. Then you start rising up. Have you not watched?—water flows downward but vapor rises upward. Exactly the same happens: unconsciousness goes downward, consciousness goes upward.

And one thing more: upward is synonymous with inward and downward is synonymous with outward. Consciousness goes inward, unconsciousness goes outward. Unconsciousness makes you interested in others—things, people, but it is always the others. Unconsciousness keeps you completely in darkness; your eyes go on being focused on others. It creates a kind of exteriority, it makes you extroverts. Consciousness creates interiority. It makes you introverts; it takes you inward, deeper and deeper.

And deeper and deeper also means higher and higher; they grow simultaneously, just as a tree grows. You only see it going upward, you don't see the roots going downward. But first the roots have to go downward, only then can the tree go upward. If a tree wants to reach the sky, then it will have to send roots to the very bottom, to the lowest depths possible. The tree grows simultaneously in both directions. In exactly the same way consciousness grows upward . . . downward, it sends its roots into your being.

14

THE ROOTS OF SUFFERING

Misery is a state of unconsciousness. We are miserable because we are not aware of what we are doing, of what we are thinking, of what we are feeling—so we are continuously contradicting ourselves each moment. Action goes in one direction, thinking goes in another, feeling is somewhere else. We go on falling apart, we become more and more fragmented. That's what misery is—we lose integration, we lose unity. We become absolutely centerless, just a periphery. And naturally a life that is not harmonious is going to be miserable, tragic, a burden to be carried somehow, a suffering. At the most one can make this suffering less painful. And there are a thousand and one kinds of painkillers available.

It is not only drugs and alcohol—the so-called religion has also functioned as opium. It drugs people. And naturally all the religions are against drugs, because they themselves deal in the same market; they are against the competitors. If people take opium, they may not be religious; there may be no need for them to be religious. They have found their opium, why should they bother about religion? And opium is cheaper, there is less involvement. If people are taking marijuana, LSD, and more refined drugs, naturally they are not going to be religious because religion is a very primitive drug. Hence all the religions are against drugs.

> We are continuously contradicting ourselves, each moment. Action goes in one direction, thinking goes in another, feeling is somewhere else. We go on falling apart, we become more and more fragmented. That's what misery is—we lose integration, we lose unity.

The reason is not that they are really against the drug. The reason is that the drugs are competitors, and of course, if people can be prevented from using drugs, they are bound to fall into the traps of the priests, because then that is the only way left. That is a way of monopolizing, so only their opium remains in the market and everything else becomes illegal.

People are living in suffering. There are only two ways out of it: They can become meditators—alert, aware, conscious . . . that's an arduous thing. It needs guts. Or the cheaper way is to find something that can make you even more unconscious than you are, so you cannot feel the misery. Find something that makes you utterly insensitive, some intoxicant, some painkiller that makes you so unconscious that you can escape into that unconsciousness and forget all about your anxiety, anguish, meaninglessness.

The second way is not the true way. The second way only makes your suffering a little more comfortable, a little more tolerable, a little more convenient. But it does not help—it does not transform you. The only transformation happens through meditation, because meditation is the only method that makes you aware. To me, meditation is the only true religion. All else is hocus-pocus. And there are different brands of opium—Christianity, Hinduism, Mohammedanism, Jainism, Buddhism—but they are just different brands. The container is different but

> The reason that religions are against drugs is that the drugs are competitors. If people can be prevented from using drugs, they are bound to fall into the traps of the priests. It is a way of monopolizing, so only their opium remains in the market and everything else becomes illegal.

the content is the same: they all help you in some way to adjust to your suffering.

My effort here is to take you beyond suffering. There is no need to adjust to suffering; there is a possibility to be totally free of suffering. But then the path is a little arduous; then the path is a challenge.

You have to become aware of your body and what you are doing with it. . . .

One day Buddha was giving his morning discourse, and the king had come to listen to him. He was sitting just in front of Buddha and was continuously moving his big toe. Buddha stopped talking and looked at the king's toe. When Buddha looked at his toe, obviously the king stopped moving it. Buddha started talking again, and again the king started moving his toe. Then Buddha asked him, "Why are you doing that?"

The king said, "Only when you stopped speaking and looked at my toe did I become aware of what I was doing; otherwise I was not at all conscious."

Buddha said, "This is your toe and you are not conscious. . . . Then you can even murder a person and you may not be conscious!"

And exactly in that way people have been murdered and the murderer has not been conscious. Many times in the courts, murderers have absolutely denied that they have murdered. First it used to be thought that they were just deceiving, but the latest findings are that they are not deceiving; they did it in an unconscious state. They were so enraged, they were so angry at that moment, that they were possessed by their rage. And when you are enraged,

> There is no need to adjust to suffering; there is a possibility to be totally free of suffering. But then the path is a little arduous; then the path is a challenge.

your body secretes certain intoxicating poisons, your blood becomes intoxicated. To be in a rage is to be in a temporary madness. And the person will completely forget about it because he was not aware at all. And that's how people are falling in love, killing each other, committing suicide, doing all kinds of things.

The first step in awareness is to be watchful of your body. Slowly, slowly one becomes alert about each gesture, each movement. And as you become aware, a miracle starts happening: many things that you used to do before simply disappear. Your body becomes more relaxed, your body becomes more attuned, a deep peace starts prevailing even in your body, a subtle music pulsates in your body.

> The first step in awareness is to be watchful of your body. And as you become aware, a miracle starts happening: many things that you used to do before simply disappear. Your body becomes more relaxed, your body becomes more attuned.

Then start becoming aware of your thoughts—the same has to be done with the thoughts. They are more subtle than the body and of course more dangerous too. And when you become aware of your thoughts, you will be surprised at what goes on inside you. If you write down whatsoever is going on at any moment, you are in for a great surprise. You will not believe it—"This is what is going on inside me?" Just for ten minutes go on writing. Close the doors, lock the doors and the windows so nobody can come in, so you can be totally honest—and light a fire so you can throw it in the fire!—so nobody will know except you. And then be truly honest; go on writing whatsoever is going on inside the mind. Don't interpret it, don't change it, don't edit it. Just put it on the paper as naked as it is, exactly as it is.

And after ten minutes read it—you

will see a mad mind inside! We are not aware that this whole madness goes on running like an undercurrent. It affects everything that is significant in your life. It affects whatsoever you are doing; it affects whatsoever you are not doing; it affects everything. And the sum total of it is going to be your life!

So this madman has to be changed. And the miracle of awareness is that you need not do anything except to become aware. The very phenomenon of watching it, changes it. Slowly, slowly, the madman disappears. Slowly, slowly, the thoughts start falling into a certain pattern: their chaos is no more, they become more of a cosmos. And then again, a deeper peace prevails.

And when your body and your mind are at peace, you will see that they are attuned to each other too, there is a bridge. Now they are not running in different directions, they are not riding on different horses. For the first time there is accord, and that accord helps immensely to work on the third step—that is, becoming aware of your feelings, emotions, moods. That is the subtlest layer and the most difficult, but if you can be aware of the thoughts, then it is just one step more. A little more intense awareness is needed as you start reflecting your moods, your emotions, your feelings.

Once you are aware of all these three, they all become joined into one phenomenon. And when all these three are one, functioning together perfectly, humming together, you can feel the music of all three—they have become an orchestra—then the fourth happens. Which you cannot do—it happens of its own accord, it is a gift from the whole. It is a reward for those who have done these three.

> When you become aware of your thoughts, you will be surprised at what goes on inside you. If you write down whatsoever is going on at any moment, you are in for a great surprise. You will not believe it!

And the fourth is the ultimate awareness that makes one awakened. One becomes aware of one's awareness—that is the fourth. That makes one a buddha, the awakened one. And only in that awakening does one come to know what bliss is. The body knows pleasure, the mind knows happiness, the heart knows joy, the fourth knows bliss. Bliss is the goal, and awareness is the path toward it.

PRIVATE WORLDS

Heraclitus says:

> Men are as forgetful and heedless
> in their waking moments
> of what is going on around them
> as they are during their sleep.
> Fools, although they hear,
> are like the deaf;
> to them the adage applies
> that whenever they are present
> they are absent.
> One should not act or speak
> as if he were asleep.
> The waking have one world in common;
> sleepers have each a private world of his own.
> Whatever we see when awake is death,
> when asleep, dreams.

Heraclitus touches the deepest problem of man, that he is fast asleep even while awake.

You sleep when you sleep, but you also sleep while you are awake. What is the meaning of it?—because this is what Buddha says, this is what Jesus says, this is what Heraclitus says. You look wide-awake, but that is only appearance; deep within you the sleep continues.

Even right now you are dreaming within. A thousand and one thoughts continue and you are not conscious of what is happening, you are not aware of what you are doing, you are not aware of who you are. You move as people move in sleep.

You must have known somebody who moves, does this or that, in sleep, and then goes back to sleep again. There is a disease called somnambulism. Many people in the night get up from their beds; their eyes are open, they can move! They can move, they can find the door. They will go to the kitchen, they will eat something; they will come back and they will go to bed. And if you ask them in the morning, they don't know anything about it. At the most, if they try to remember it, they will see that they had a dream that night, that they woke up, they went into the kitchen. But it was a dream, at the most; even that is difficult to remember.

> What have you done in your past? Can you exactly recollect it, why you did what you did? What happened to you? Were you alert when it was happening?

Many people have committed crimes; many murderers when in the court say that they don't know, they don't remember ever having done such a thing. It is not that they are deceiving the court—no. Now psychoanalysts have come to find that they are not deceiving, they are not being untrue; they are absolutely truthful. They did commit the murder—when they were fast asleep they did commit it—as if in a dream. This sleep is deeper than ordinary sleep. This sleep is like being drunk: you can move a little, you can do a little, you can be a little aware also—but drunk. You don't know what exactly is happening. What have you done in your past? Can you exactly recollect it, why you did what you did? What happened to you? Were you alert when it was happening? You fall in love not knowing why; you become angry not knowing why. You find excuses, of course; you rationalize whatsoever you do—but rationalization is not awareness.

Awareness means that whatsoever is happening in the moment is happening with complete consciousness; you are present there. If you are present when anger is happening, anger cannot happen. It can happen only when you are fast asleep. When you are present, immediate transformation starts in your being, because when you are present, aware, many things are simply not possible. All that is called sin is not possible if you are aware. So, in fact, there is only one sin, and that is unawareness.

> The original word *sin* means to miss. It doesn't mean to commit something wrong, it simply means to miss, to be absent, to do something without being present—this is the only sin.

The original word *sin* means to miss. It doesn't mean to commit something wrong; it simply means to miss, to be absent. The Hebrew root for the word *sin* means to miss. That exists in a few English words: *mis*conduct, *mis*behavior. To miss means not to be there, doing something without being present—this is the only sin. And the only virtue? While you are doing something, you are fully alert—what Gurdjieff calls self-remembering, what Buddha calls being rightly mindful, what Krishnamurti calls awareness, what Kabir has called *surati*. To be there!—that's all that is needed, nothing more.

You need not change anything, and even if you try to change, you cannot. You have been trying to change many things in you. Have you succeeded? How many times have you decided not to be angry again?

What happened to your decision? When the moment comes, you are again in the same trap: you become angry, and after the anger has gone, again you repent. It has become a vicious circle: you commit anger and then you repent, then you are ready again to commit it.

Remember, even while you are repenting, you are not there; that repentance is also part of sin. That's why nothing happens. You go on trying and trying, and you make many decisions and you take many vows, but nothing happens—you remain the same. You are exactly the same as when you were born, not even a slight change has happened in you. Not that you have not tried, not that you have not tried enough, you have tried and tried and tried. And you fail because it is not a question of effort. More effort won't help. It is a question of being alert, not of effort.

If you are alert, many things simply drop; you need not drop them. In awareness, certain things are not possible. And this is my definition, there is no other criterion. You cannot fall in love if you are aware; then falling in love is a sin. You can love, but it will not be like a fall, it will be like a rise. Why do we use the term *falling in love*? It is a falling; you are falling, you are not rising. When you are aware, falling is not possible—not even in love. It is not possible; it is simply not possible. With awareness, it is impossible; you rise in love. And rising in love is a totally different phenomenon from falling in love. Falling in love is a dream state. That's why people who are in love, you can see it from their eyes: as if they are more asleep than others, intoxicated, dreaming. You can see from their eyes because their eyes have a sleepiness. People who rise in love are totally dif-

> You cannot fall in love if you are aware; then falling in love is a sin. You can love, but it will not be like a fall, it will be like a rise.

ferent. You can see they are no longer in a dream, they are facing the reality and they are growing through it.

Falling in love you remain a child; rising in love you mature. And by and by love becomes not a relationship, it becomes a state of your being. Then it is not that you love this and you don't love that, no—you are simply love. Whosoever comes near you, you share with them. Whatsoever is happening, you give your love to it. You touch a rock and you touch as if you are touching your beloved's body. You look at the tree and you look as if you are looking at your beloved's face. It becomes a state of being. Not that you are in love— now you *are* love. This is rising, this is not falling.

Love is beautiful when you rise through it, and love becomes dirty and ugly when you fall through it. And sooner or later you will find that it proves poisonous, it becomes a bondage. You have been caught in it, your freedom has been crushed. Your wings have been cut; now you are free no more. Falling in love you become a possession: you possess and you allow somebody to possess you. You become a thing, and you try to convert the other person you have fallen in love with into a thing.

Look at a husband and a wife: they both have become like things, they are persons no more. Both are trying to possess each other. Only things can be possessed, persons never. How can you possess a person? How can you dominate a person? How can you convert a person into a possession? Impossible! But the husband is trying to possess the wife; the wife is trying the same. Then there is a clash, then they both become basically enemies. Then they are destructive to each other.

It happened:

Mulla Nasruddin walked into the office of a cemetery and complained to the manager: "I know well that my wife is buried here in your cemetery, but I can't find her grave."

The manager checked in his register and asked, "What is her name?"

So Mulla said, "Mrs. Mulla Nasruddin."

The manager looked again and said, "There is no Mrs. Mulla Nasruddin, but there is a Mulla Nasruddin. We are sorry, it seems something has gone wrong in the register."

Nasruddin said, "Nothing is wrong. Where is the grave of Mulla Nasruddin?—because everything is in my name."

Even the grave of his wife!

Possession . . . everybody goes on trying to possess the beloved, the lover. This is no longer love. In fact, when you possess a person, you hate, you destroy, you kill; you are a murderer. Love should give freedom; love *is* freedom. Love will make the beloved more and more free, love will give wings, and love will open the vast sky. It cannot become a prison, an enclosure. But that love you don't know, because that happens only when you are aware; that quality of love comes only when there is awareness. You know a love that is a sin, because it comes out of sleep.

And this is so for everything you do. Even if you try to do something good, you harm. Look at the do-gooders: they always do harm, they are the most mischievous people in the world. Social reformers, so-called revolutionaries, they are the most mischievous people. But it is difficult to see where their mischief lies because they are good people, they are always doing good to others—that is their way of creating an imprisonment for the other. If you allow them to do something good to you, you will be possessed. They start by massaging your feet, and sooner or later you

> Love will make the beloved more and more free, love will give wings, and love will open the vast sky. It cannot become a prison, an enclosure. But that quality of love comes only when there is awareness.

> ❧
>
> Priests have done so well because they converted freedom into imprisonments, they converted truth into dogmas—they converted everything from the plane of awareness to the plane of sleep.

will find their hands reach your neck! At the feet they start, at the neck they end, because they are unaware; they don't know what they are doing. They have learned a trick—if you want to possess someone, do good. They are not even conscious that they have learned this trick. But they will do harm because anything—anything—that tries to possess the other person, whatsoever its name or form, is irreligious, is a sin.

Your churches, your temples, your mosques, they have all committed sins toward you because they all became possessors, they all became dominations. Every church is against religion—because religion is freedom! Why does it happen then? Jesus tries to give freedom, wings to you. Then what happens, how does this church come in? It happens because Jesus lives on a totally different plane of being, the plane of awareness; and those who listen to him, those who follow him, they live on the plane of sleep. Whatsoever they hear, interpret, it is interpreted through their own dreams. And whatsoever they create is going to be a sin. Christ gives you religion, and then people who are fast asleep convert it into a church.

It is said that once Satan, the devil, was sitting under a tree, very sad. A saint was passing; he looked at Satan and said, "We have heard that you never rest, you are always doing some mischief or other somewhere or other. What are you doing here sitting under the tree?"

Satan was really depressed. He said, "It seems my work has been taken over by the priests, and I cannot do anything—I am completely unemployed. Sometimes I have the idea of committing suicide because these priests are doing so well."

Priests have done so well because they converted freedom into imprisonments, they converted truth into dogmas—they converted everything from the plane of awareness to the plane of sleep.

Try to understand exactly what this sleep is, because if you can feel what it is, you have already started to become alert—already you are on the way out of it. What is this sleep? How does it happen? What is the mechanism? What is its modus operandi?

The mind is always either in the past or in the future. It cannot be in the present, it is absolutely impossible for the mind to be in the present. When you are in the present, the mind is there no more—because mind means thinking. How can you think in the present? You can think about the past; it has already become part of the memory, the mind can work it out. You can think about the future; it is not yet there, the mind can dream about it. Mind can do two things. Either it can move into the past—there is space enough to move, the vast space of the past; you can go on and on and on—or the mind can move into the future; again vast space, no end to it, you can imagine and imagine and dream. But how can mind function in the present? It has no space for the mind to make any movement.

The present is just a dividing line, that's all. It has no space. It divides the past and the future—just a dividing line. You can *be* in

> You can *be* in the present but you cannot think, for thinking, space is needed. Thoughts need space, they are just like things. Remember it—thoughts are subtle things, they are material. The dimension of the spiritual starts only when there are no thoughts.

the present but you cannot think; for thinking, space is needed. Thoughts need space, they are just like things. Remember it—thoughts are subtle things, they are material. Thoughts are not spiritual, because the dimension of the spiritual starts only when there are no thoughts. Thoughts are material things, very subtle, and every material thing needs space.

You cannot be thinking in the present. The moment you start thinking, it is already the past. You see the sun is rising; you see it and you say, "What a beautiful sunrise!"—it is already the past. When the sun is rising, there is not even space enough to say "How beautiful!" because when you utter these two words—"How beautiful!"—the experience has already become past; the mind already knows it in the memory. But *exactly* when the sun is rising, exactly when the sun is on the rise, how can you think? What can you think? You can *be with* the rising sun, but you cannot think. For *you* there is enough space—but not for thoughts.

A beautiful flower in the garden and you say, "A beautiful rose"—now you are not with this rose, this moment; it is already a memory. When the flower is there and you are there, both present to each other, how can you think? What can you think? How is thinking possible? There is no space for it. The space is so narrow—in fact there is no space at all—that you and the flower cannot even exist as two because there is not enough space for two, only one can exist.

That's why in a deep presence you are the flower and the flower has become you. When there is no thinking, who is the flower and who is the one who is observing? The observer becomes the observed. Suddenly boundaries are lost. Suddenly you have penetrated, penetrated into the flower and the flower has penetrated into you. Suddenly you are not two—one exists.

If you start thinking, you have become two again. If you don't think, where is the duality? When you exist with the flower, not thinking, it is a dialogue—not a duologue but a dialogue. When you exist with your lover, it is a dialogue, not a duologue, because the two are not there. Sitting by the side of your lover, holding the hand of your beloved, you simply exist. You don't think of the days past and gone; you don't think of the future coming—you are here, now. And it is so beautiful to be here and now, and so intense, no thought can penetrate this intensity.

And narrow is the gate; narrow is the gate of the present. Not even two can enter into it together, only one. In the present, thinking is not possible, dreaming is not possible, because dreaming is nothing but thinking in pictures. Both are things, both are material.

When you are in the present without thinking, you are for the first time spiritual. A new dimension opens—that dimension is awareness. Because you have not known that dimension, Heraclitus will say you are asleep, you are not aware. Awareness means to be in the moment so totally that there is no movement toward the past, no movement toward the future—all movement stops.

That doesn't mean that you become static. A new movement starts, a movement in depth. There are two types of movement, and that is the meaning of Jesus' cross: it shows two movements, a crossroads. One movement is linear: you move in a line, from one thing to another, from one thought to another. From one dream to another dream— from A you move to B, from B you move to C, from C you move to D. This way you move, in a line, horizontal. This is the movement of time; this is the movement of one who is fast asleep. You can go like a shuttle, back and forth—the line is there. You can come from B to A, or you can go from A to B—the line is there.

There is another movement, which is in a totally different dimension. That movement is not horizontal, it is ver-

> Awareness means to be in the moment so totally that there is no movement toward the past, no movement toward the future—all movement stops.

> ❧
>
> If you move from one thought to another, you remain in the world of time. If you move into the moment—not into thought—you move into eternity. You are not static, nothing is static in this world, nothing can be static—but a new movement arises, a movement without motivation.

tical. You don't go from A to B, from B to C; you go from A to a deeper A: from A1 to A2, A3, A4, in depth—or in height.

When thinking stops, the new movement starts. Now you fall into depth, in an abysslike phenomenon. People who are meditating deeply, they come to that point sooner or later; then they become afraid because they feel as if an abyss has opened—bottomless, you feel dizzy, you become afraid. You would like to cling to the old movement because it was known; this feels like death.

That is the meaning of Jesus' cross: it is a death. Going from the horizontal to the vertical is death—that is the real death. But it is death only from one side; on the other side it is resurrection. It is dying in order to be born; it is dying from one dimension to be born in another dimension. Horizontal you are Jesus. Vertical you become Christ.

If you move from one thought to another, you remain in the world of time. If you move into the moment—not into thought—you move into eternity. You are not static; nothing is static in this world, nothing can be static—but a new movement arises, a movement without motivation. Remember these words. On the horizontal line you move because of motivation. You have to achieve something—money, prestige, power, or God, but you have to achieve something. A motivation is there.

A motivated movement means sleep. An unmotivated movement means awareness—you move because to move is sheer joy, you move because movement is life, you move because life is energy and energy is movement. You move because energy is delight—not for anything else. There is no goal to it, you are not after some achievement. In fact you are not going anywhere, you are not going at all—you are simply delighting in the energy. There is no goal outside the movement itself; movement has its own intrinsic value, no extrinsic value.

A buddha also lives—a Heraclitus lives; I am here living, breathing—but with a different type of movement, unmotivated.

Somebody was asking me a few days ago, "Why do you help people in meditation?"

I told him, "This is my delight. There is no why to it—I simply enjoy." Just as a person enjoys planting seeds in the garden, waiting for the flowers—when you flower, I enjoy. It is gardening; when somebody flowers, it is a sheer delight. And I share. There is no goal to it. If you fail, I am not going to be frustrated. If you don't flower, that too is okay, because flowering cannot be forced. You cannot open a bud forcibly—you can, but then you kill it. It may look like a flowering; it is not a flowering.

The whole world moves, existence moves, into eternity. Mind moves in time. Existence is moving into the depth and the height, and mind moves backward and forward. Mind moves horizontally— that is sleep. If you can move vertically, that is awareness.

Be in the moment. Bring your total being into the moment. Don't allow the past to interfere and don't allow the future to come in. The past is no more, it is dead. And as Jesus says, "Let the dead bury their dead." The past is no more, why are you worried about it? Why do you go on chewing it again and again and again? Are you mad? It is no more; it is just in your mind, it is just a memory. The future is not yet—what are you doing thinking about the future? That which is not yet, how can you think about it? What can you plan about it? Whatsoever you do about it is not going to happen, and then you will be frustrated, because the whole has its own plan. Why do you try to have your own plans against it?

The existence has its own plans, it is wiser than you—the whole has to be wiser than the part. Why are you pretending to be the whole? The whole has its own destiny, its own fulfillment; why do you bother about it? And whatsoever you do will be a sin because you will be missing the moment—this moment. And if it becomes a habit—as it becomes; if you start missing, it becomes a habitual form—then when the future has come again, you will be missing it because it will not be a future when it comes, it will be a present. Yesterday you were thinking about today because then it was tomorrow; now it is today and you are thinking about tomorrow, and when the tomorrow comes, it will become today—because anything that exists, exists here and now, it cannot exist otherwise. And if you have a fixed mode of functioning such that your mind always looks at tomorrow, then when will you live? Tomorrow never comes. Then you will go on missing—and this is sin. This is the meaning of the Hebrew root of *to sin*.

The moment the future enters, time enters. You have sinned against existence, you have missed. And this has become a fixed pattern: robotlike, you go on missing.

I have people coming to me from faraway countries. When they are there, they think about me and they get excited about me, and they read and they think and they dream. When they come here, they start thinking about their homes; the moment they arrive, they are already going back! Then they start thinking about their children, their wives, and their jobs and this and that and a thousand and one things. And I see the whole foolishness. Again they will be back there and then they will be thinking about me. They miss, and this is sin.

While you are here with me, be here with me—be totally here with me so that you can learn a new mode of movement, so that you can move into eternity, not in time.

Time is the world and eternity is God; horizontal is the world, vertical is God. Both meet at a point—that is where Jesus is crucified. Both meet, the horizontal and the vertical, at a point—that point is here and now. From here and now you can go on two journeys: one journey in the world, in the future; the other journey into God, into depth.

Become more and more aware, become more and more alert and sensitive to the present.

What will you do? How can it become possible?—because you are so fast asleep that you can make that a dream also. You can make that itself a thinking object, a thinking process. You can become so tense about it that just because of it you cannot be in the present. If you think too much about how to be in the present, this thinking won't help. If you feel too much guilt . . . if you sometimes move into the past—you will; it has been such a long routine, and sometimes you will start thinking about the future—immediately you will feel guilty that you have committed a sin again.

Don't become guilty. Understand the sin, but don't become guilty—and this is very, very delicate. If you become guilty, you have missed the whole thing. Now, in a new way the old pattern starts. Now you feel guilty because you have missed the present. Now you are thinking about the past—because that present is no longer present; it is past, and you are feeling guilty about it. You are still missing.

So remember one thing: whenever you realize that you have gone to the past or into the future, don't create a problem out of it. Simply come to the present, not creating any problem. It's okay! Simply bring back your awareness. You will miss millions of times; it is not going to happen right now, immediately. It can happen, but it cannot happen because of you. It is such a long, long, fixed mode of behavior that you cannot change it right now. But no worry, existence is not in a hurry. Eternity can wait eternally. Don't create a tension about it.

Whenever you feel you have missed, come back, that's all. Don't feel guilty; that's a trick of the mind, now it is again playing a game. Don't repent: "I again forgot." Just when you think, come back to whatsoever you are doing. Taking your bath, come back; eating your food, come back; going for a walk, come back. The moment you feel you are not here and now, come back—simply, innocently. Don't create guilt. If you become guilty, then you miss the point.

There is sin, and there is no guilt—but that's difficult for you. If you feel there is something wrong, you become immediately guilty. The mind is very, very cunning. If you become guilty, the game has started now—on new ground, but the game is old. People come to me, they say, "We go on forgetting." They are so sad when they say, "We go on forgetting. We try but we remember only for a few seconds. We remain alert, self-remembering, then again it is lost— what to do?" Nothing can be done! It is not a question of doing at all. What can you do? The only thing that can be done is not to create guilt. Simply come back.

The more you come back . . . simply, remember. Not with a serious face, not with much effort—simply, innocently, not creating a problem out of it. Because eternity has no problems—all problems exist on the horizontal plane; this problem will also exist on the horizontal plane. The vertical plane knows no problems. It is sheer delight, without any anxiety, without any anguish, without any worry, any guilt, nothing. Be simple and come back.

You will miss many times, it is taken for granted. But don't worry about it; that is how it is. You will miss many times, but that is not the point. Don't pay much attention to the fact that you have missed many times, pay much attention to the fact that you have regained many times. Remember this—the emphasis should not be that you missed many times, it should be that you regained remembrance many times. Feel happy about it. That you miss, of course, is as it should be. You are human, have lived on the horizontal plane for many, many lives, so it is natural. The beauty is that many times you came back. You have done the impossible; feel happy about it!

In twenty-four hours, twenty-four thousand times you will miss, but twenty-four thousand times you will regain. Now a new mode will start functioning. So many times you come back home; now a new dimension is breaking in, by and by. More and more you will be able to stay in awareness, less and less you will go back and forth. The span of going back and forth will be smaller and smaller. Less and less you will forget, more and more you will remember—you are entering the vertical. Suddenly one day, the horizontal disappears. An intensity comes to awareness and the horizontal disappears.

That is the meaning behind Shankara, Vedanta, and Hindus calling this world illusory. Because when awareness becomes perfect, this world—this world that you have created out of your mind—simply disappears; another world becomes revealed to you. *Maya* disappears, the illusion disappears—the illusion is there because of your sleep, your unconsciousness.

It is just like a dream. In the night you move in a dream, and when the dream is there, it is so true. Have you ever thought in a dream, "This is not possible"? The impossible happens in a dream, but you cannot doubt it. In a dream you have such faith; in a dream nobody is skeptical, not even a Bertrand Russell. No, in a dream everybody is like a child, trusting whatsoever happens. You see your wife coming in a dream—suddenly she becomes a horse. Not for a single moment do you say, "How can this be possible?"

Dream is trust, it is faith. You cannot doubt in a dream. Once you start doubting in a dream the rules are broken. Once you doubt, the dream starts disappearing. If even once you can remember that this is a dream, suddenly this will become a shock and the dream will shatter and you will be fully awake.

> This world that you see around you is not the real world. Not that it doesn't exist—it exists—but you are seeing it through a screen of sleep. An unconsciousness is in between, you look at it, you interpret it in your own way.

This world that you see around you is not the real world. Not that it doesn't exist—it exists—but you are seeing it through a screen of sleep. An unconsciousness is in between; you look at it, you interpret it in your own way; you are just like a drunkard.

It happened:

Mulla Nasruddin came running. He was totally drunk, and the man who was operating the elevator was just going to close the door, but Mulla somehow pushed in. It was overcrowded. Everybody became aware that Mulla was very drunk; his breath was smelling. He tried to pretend; he tried to face toward the door, but he couldn't see anything—his eyes too were drunk and sleepy. Somehow he was trying to stand, but that was not possible either. And then he felt embarrassed, because everybody was looking and everybody was thinking that he was completely drunk; he could feel that. Not knowing what else to do, he suddenly said, "You must be wondering why I called this meeting."

By the morning Nasruddin will be okay. He will laugh, as you are laughing.

All buddhas have laughed when they awaken. Their laughter is like a lion's roar. They laugh, not at you—they laugh at the whole cosmic joke. They lived in a dream, in sleep, intoxicated completely by desire, and through desire they looked at existence. Then it was not the real existence; they projected their own sleep on it.

You are taking the whole existence as a screen, and then you project your own mind on it. You see things that are not there, and you don't see things that are there. And the mind has explanations for everything. If you raise a doubt, the mind explains. It creates theories, philosophies, systems, just to feel comfortable that nothing is wrong. All philosophies exist to make life convenient, so that everything looks okay, nothing is wrong—but everything is wrong while you are asleep.

One man came to me. He was worried; he is the father of a beautiful daughter. He was very much worried; he said, "Every morning she feels a little sick, and I have been to all the doctors and they say nothing is wrong. So what to do?"

So I told him, "You go to Mulla Nasruddin—he is the wise guy around here and he knows everything, because I have never heard him say, 'I don't know.' You go."

He went. I also followed just to see what Nasruddin would say. Nasruddin closed his eyes, contemplated the problem, then opened his eyes and said, "Do you give her milk before she goes to bed at night?"

The man said, "Yes!"

Nasruddin said, "Now, I have found the problem: if you give milk to a child, then the child changes sides the whole night from right to left, from left to right, and through the churning the milk becomes curd. Then the curd becomes cheese, then the cheese becomes butter, then the butter becomes fat, then the fat becomes sugar, then the sugar becomes alcohol—and, of course, in the morning she has a hangover."

This is what all the philosophies are: some explanations of things, some explanation of things that cannot be explained, pretending to know about something that is not known. But they make life convenient. You can sleep better, they are like tranquilizers.

Remember, this is the difference between philosophy and religiousness: philosophy is a tranquilizer, religiousness is a shock; philosophy helps you to sleep well, religiousness brings you out of sleep. Religiousness is not a philosophy—it is a technique to bring you out of your unconsciousness. And all philosophies are techniques to help you to sleep well; they give you dreams, utopias.

Religiousness takes all dreams from you, all utopias. Religiousness brings you to the truth—and the truth is possible only when you are not dreaming. A dreaming mind cannot see the true. A dreaming mind will convert the truth also into a dream.

Have you ever observed it? You set an alarm; in the morning you want to get up at four o'clock, you have to catch a train. Then in the morning the alarm goes off, and your mind creates a dream: you are sitting in a temple and the bells of the temple are tolling—then everything is explained. The alarm is no longer a problem, it cannot awaken you. You have explained it away—immediately!

Mind is subtle. And now psychoanalysts are puzzled as to how it happens, how the mind creates explanations immediately, so immediately. It is so difficult!—the mind must project it beforehand. How, suddenly, do you find yourself in a church or in a temple where the bells are tolling? The alarm goes off and immediately you have an explanation within the dream. You are trying to avoid the alarm; you don't want to get up, you don't want to get up on such a cold winter night. The mind says, "This is not the alarm, this is a temple you are visiting." Everything explained, you continue to sleep.

This is what philosophies have been doing, and that's why there are so many philosophies—because everybody needs a different explanation. The explanation that helps somebody else to go into sleep will not help you. And this is what Heraclitus says in this passage.

Now try to understand him. He says:

> Men are as forgetful and heedless
> in their waking moments
> of what is going on around them
> as they are during their sleep.

In sleep you are not aware of what goes on around you, but in your waking hours are you aware of what goes on around you?

Much research has been done. Ninety-eight percent of messages coming to you, your mind never allows to enter—98 percent. Only 2 percent are allowed to enter, and that 2 percent the mind also interprets. I say something, you hear something else. I say something else, you interpret it in such a way that it doesn't disturb your sleep. Your mind immediately gives you an interpretation. You find a place in your mind for it, and the mind absorbs it; it becomes part of the mind. That's why you go on missing Buddhas, Christs, Heraclituses, and others. They go on talking to you; they go on saying they have found something, they have experienced something, but when they say it to you, you immediately interpret it. You have your own tricks.

Aristotle was very much disturbed by Heraclitus. He decided that this man must have some defect in his character. Finished!—you have categorized him because he doesn't suit you, he disturbs you. Heraclitus must have been very heavy on Aristotle's mind—because Aristotle moves on the horizontal, he is the master of that, and this man Heraclitus is trying to push you into the abyss. Aristotle moves on the plain ground of logic, and this man Heraclitus is trying to push you into the mystery. Some explanation is needed. Says Aristotle, "This man has some defect—biological, physiological, 'characterological,' some defect is there. Otherwise, why should he insist on paradox? Why should he insist on mystery? Why should he insist that there exists a harmony between the opposites? Opposites are opposites; there is no harmony. Life is life and death is death—be clear about it, don't mix things. This man seems to be a muddler."

Lao Tzu also was the same. Lao Tzu said, "Everybody seems to be wise except me. Everybody seems to be very clever except me—I am a fool!" Lao Tzu is one of the greatest, one of the most wise persons ever born, but he feels amidst you that he is a fool. Lao Tzu says, "Everybody seems to be so clear a thinker, I am muddleheaded." What Aristotle says to Heraclitus, Lao Tzu says about himself.

Lao Tzu says, "When somebody listens to my teaching without the mind, he becomes enlightened. If somebody listens to my teaching through the mind, then he finds his own explanations, which have nothing to do with me. And when somebody listens, not listening at all—there are people who listen without listening—when somebody listens as if he is listening without listening, then he laughs at my foolishness." And the third type of mind is the majority. Says Lao Tzu, "If the majority doesn't laugh at you, be aware that you must be saying something wrong. If the majority laughs, only then are you saying something true. When the majority thinks you are a fool, only then is there some possibility of your being a wise man; otherwise, there is no possibility."

Heraclitus looks muddleheaded to Aristotle. It will look so to you, also, because Aristotle has captured all the universities, all the colleges of the whole world. Now everywhere you are taught logic, not mystery. Everywhere you are taught to be rational, not mystical. Everybody is being trained to be clear-cut. If you want to be clear-cut, you have to move on the horizontal. There, A is A, B is B, and A is never B. But in the mysterious abyss of the vertical, boundaries meet and merge into each other. Man is woman, woman is man; right is wrong, wrong is right; dark is light, light is dark; life is death, death is life. All boundaries meet and merge.

> Aristotle has captured all the universities, all the colleges of the whole world. Now everywhere you are taught logic, not mystery.

Hence, God is a mystery, not a syllogism. Those who give proofs for God are simply doing the impossible; no proof can be given for God. Proofs exist on the horizontal.

That is the meaning of trust: you fall into the abyss, you experience the abyss, you simply disappear in it . . . and you know. You know only when the mind is not, never before.

Wherever you are present, that is exactly the place where you are absent. You may be somewhere else, but not there, where you are. Wherever you are, there you are not.

It is said in old Tibetan scriptures that God comes many times to you but he never finds you there, where you are. He knocks at your door, but the host is not there—he is always somewhere else. Are you in your house, at your home, or somewhere else? How can God find you? No need to go to him, just be at home and he will find you. He is in search of you just as you are in search of him. Just be at home so, when he comes, he can find you. He comes, he knocks, millions of times, waits at the door, but you are never there.

Says Heraclitus:

> *Fools, although they hear,*
> *are like the deaf;*
> *to them the adage applies*
> *that whenever they are present*
> *they are absent.*

This is the sleep: being absent, being not present to the present moment, being somewhere else.

It happened:

Mulla Nasruddin was sitting in the coffeehouse and talking about his generosity. And when he talks, he goes to the very extreme, as everybody does, because he forgets what he is saying. Then somebody said, "Nasruddin, if you are so generous, why do you never invite us to your home? Not even for a single meal have you invited us. So what about it?"

Nasruddin was so excited he forgot completely about his wife. So he said, "Come on, right now!" The nearer he reached home, the more sober he became. Then he remembered his wife and became afraid—thirty persons coming. Just outside the house he said, "You wait! You all know I have a wife. You also have wives so you know. Just wait. Let me first go and persuade her, then I will call you in." So he went and disappeared.

They waited and they waited and they waited and he did not come, did not come, so they knocked. Nasruddin had told his wife exactly what had happened, that he was talking too much about generosity and he had been caught. His wife said, "But we don't have anything for thirty persons, and nothing is possible at this late hour in the night."

So Nasruddin said, "You do one thing: when they knock, you simply go and tell them that Nasruddin is not at home."

So when they knocked, the wife came and said, "Nasruddin is not at home."

They said, "This is surprising because we came with him, and he went in and we have not seen him go out, and we are waiting on the step, thirty persons—he must be in. You go in and find him. He must be hiding somewhere."

His wife went in. She said, "What to do?"

Nasruddin became excited. He said, "Wait!" He came out and said, "What do you mean? He could have gone out by the back door!"

This is possible, this is happening every day to you. Nasruddin forgot himself completely; that's what happened—in the logic he forgot himself. The logic is right, the argument is right, but . . . "What do you mean? You are waiting at the front door; he could have gone by the back door"—the logic is right, but Nasruddin has completely forgotten that he himself is saying it.

You are not present. You are neither in the present to the world nor to yourself. This is the sleep. Then how can you hear? Then how can you see? Then how can you feel? If you are not present here and now, then all doors are

> Eyes are just windows, they can't see unless you see through them. How can a window see? You have to stand at the window, only then can you see.

closed. You are a dead person, you are not alive. That's why Jesus again and again says to his hearers, listeners: "If you have ears, hear me; if you have eyes, see me!"

Heraclitus must have found many people who listen but don't hear, who see but can't see, because their homes are completely empty. The master is not at home. Eyes are looking, ears are hearing, but the master is not present inside. Eyes are just windows; they can't see unless you see through them. How can a window see? You have to stand at the window, only then can you see. How?—it is just a window, it cannot feel. If you are there, then it becomes totally different.

> Control is a poor substitute for awareness, a very poor substitute; it doesn't help much. If you are aware, you need not control anger; in awareness, anger never arises. They cannot exist together.

The whole body is like a house and the mind is traveling; the master is always traveling somewhere else and the house remains empty. And the life knocks at your door—you may call it God or whatsoever you like, the name doesn't matter; call it existence—it knocks at the door, it is already knocking continuously, but you are never found there. This is the sleep.

One should not act or speak
as if he were asleep.

Act, speak, with full awareness and then you will find a tremendous change in you. The very fact that you are aware changes your acts. Then you cannot commit sin. Not that you have to control yourself, no! Control is a poor substitute for awareness, a very poor substitute; it doesn't help much. If you are aware, you need not control anger; in awareness, anger never arises. They cannot exist

> Acts don't mean anything. Acts do not matter—you, your awareness, your being conscious, mindful, is what matters. What you do is not the concern.

together; there is no coexistence for them. In awareness, jealousy never arises. In awareness, many things simply disappear—all the things that are negative.

It is just like a light. When the light is in your house, how can darkness exist there? It simply escapes. When your house is lighted, how can you stumble? How can you knock at the wall? The light is there, you know the door; you simply reach the door, you get out or in. When there is darkness, you stumble, you grope, you fall. When you are unaware, you grope, you stumble, you fall. Anger is nothing but stumbling; jealousy is nothing but groping in the dark. All that is wrong is wrong, not because of itself but because you are living in darkness.

If a Jesus wants to be angry, he can be; he can use it. You cannot use it—you are being used by it. If Jesus feels that it will be good and helpful, he can use anything—he is a master. Jesus can be angry without being angry. Many people worked with Gurdjieff, and he was a terrible man. When he was angry, he would be terribly angry, he would look like a murderer! But that was just a game, just a situation to help somebody. And immediately, not a single moment's gap would be there, he would look at another person and he would be smiling. And he would look again at the same person toward whom he had been angry, and he would be angry and terrible looking.

It is possible. When you are aware, you can use everything. Even poison becomes elixir when you are aware. And when you are asleep, even elixir becomes poison—because the whole thing depends on your being alert or not. Acts don't mean anything. Acts do not matter—you, your awareness, your being conscious, mindful, is what matters. What you do is not the concern.

It happened:

There was one great master, a Buddhist master, Nagarjuna. A thief came to him. The thief had fallen in love with the master because he had never seen such a beautiful person, such infinite grace. He asked Nagarjuna, "Is there some possibility of my growth also? But one thing I must make clear to you: I am a thief. And another thing: I cannot leave it, so please don't make it a condition. I will do whatsoever you say, but I cannot stop being a thief. That I have tried many times—it never works, so I have left the whole sport. I have accepted my destiny, that I am going to be a thief and remain a thief, so don't talk about it. From the very beginning let it be clear."

Nagarjuna said, "Why are you afraid? Who is going to talk about your being a thief?"

The thief said, "But whenever I go to a monk, to a religious priest, or to a religious saint, they always say, 'First stop stealing.'"

Nagarjuna laughed and said, "Then you must have gone to thieves; otherwise, why? Why should they be concerned? I am not concerned!"

The thief was very happy. He said, "Then it is okay. It seems that now I can become a disciple. You are the right master."

Nagarjuna accepted him and said, "Now you can go and do whatsoever you like. Only one condition has to be followed: be aware! Go, break into houses, enter, take things, steal; do whatsoever you like, that is of no concern to me, I am not a thief—but do it with full awareness."

The thief couldn't understand that he was falling into the trap. He said, "Then everything is okay. I will try."

After three weeks he came back and said, "You are tricky—because if I become aware, I cannot steal. If I steal, awareness disappears. I am in a fix."

45

Nagarjuna said, "No more talk about your being a thief and stealing. I am not concerned; I am not a thief. Now, you decide! If you want awareness, then you decide. If you don't want it, then too you decide."

The man said, "But now it is difficult. I have tasted it a little, and it is so beautiful—I will leave anything, whatsoever you say. Just the other night for the first time I was able to enter the palace of the king. I opened the treasure. I could have become the richest man in the world—but you were following me and I had to be aware. When I became aware, suddenly—no motivation, no desire. When I became aware, diamonds looked just like stones, ordinary stones. When I lost awareness, the treasure was there. And I waited and did this many times. I would become aware and I became like a buddha, and I could not even touch it because the whole thing looked foolish, stupid—just stones, what am I doing? Losing myself for stones? But then I would lose awareness; they would become again beautiful, the whole illusion. But finally I decided that they were not worth it."

Once you have known awareness, nothing is worth it—you have known the greatest bliss of life. Then, suddenly, many things simply drop; they become stupid, become foolish. The motivation is not there, the desire is not there, the dreams have fallen.

One should not act or speak
as if he were asleep.

This is the only key.

The waking have one world in common;
sleepers have each a private world of his own.

Dreams are private, absolutely private! Nobody can enter into your dream. You cannot share a dream with your beloved. Husbands and wives, they sleep on one bed but dream separately. It is impossible to share a dream because it is nothing—how can you share a nothing? Just like a bubble, it is absolutely nonexistential; you cannot share it, you have to dream alone.

That's why—because of sleepers, so many sleepers—there exist so many worlds. You have your own world; if you are asleep you live enclosed in your own thoughts, concepts, dreams, desires. Whenever you meet another, two worlds clash. Worlds in collision—this is what the situation is. Watch!

Look at a husband and a wife talking; they are not talking at all. The husband is thinking about the office, the salary; the wife is thinking about her dresses for Christmas. Inside they have their own private worlds, but their private worlds meet somewhere—clash, rather—because the wife's dresses will depend on the salary of the husband, and the husband's salary has to provide for the wife's dresses. The wife says "darling," but behind the word *darling* are dresses; she is thinking about them. The "darling" doesn't mean that which is written in the dictionary, because every time a woman says "darling" this is now just a facade, and the husband immediately becomes afraid. He does not show it, of course, because when someone says "darling" you cannot show it. He says, "What is it, dear? How are you?" But he is afraid because he is thinking of his salary, and he knows Christmas is coming and there is danger.

> If you are asleep, you live enclosed in your own thoughts, concepts, dreams, desires. Whenever you meet another, two worlds clash. Worlds in collision— this is what the situation is.

Mulla Nasruddin's wife was saying to him, "What has happened? Lately I even cry and weep and tears roll down my face and you don't even ask, 'Why are you weeping?' "

Nasruddin said, "Enough is enough!—it costs too much to ask. And in the past I have committed that mistake so many times, because those tears are not just tears—dresses, a new house, new furniture, a new car, many things are hidden behind those tears. Those tears are just a start."

No dialogue is possible because there are two private worlds inside. Only conflict is possible.

Dreams are private, truth is not private. Truth cannot be private—truth cannot be mine or yours, truth cannot be Christian or Hindu, truth cannot be Indian or Greek. Truth cannot be private.

Dreams are private. Whatsoever is private, remember, it must belong to the world of dreams. Truth is an open sky; it is for all, it is one.

That's why when Lao Tzu speaks, the language may be different; Buddha talks, the language is different; Heraclitus talks, the language is different—but they mean the same, they indicate toward the same. They don't live in private worlds. The private world has disappeared with their dreams, desires—with the mind. Mind has a private world but consciousness has no private worlds. The waking have one world in common. . . . All those who are waking, they have one world in common—that is existence. And all those who are asleep and dreaming have their own worlds.

Your world has to be dropped; that is the only renunciation I require of you. I don't say leave your wife, I don't say leave your

> Dreams are private. Whatsoever is private, remember, it must belong to the world of dreams. Truth is an open sky, it is for all, it is one.

job, I don't say leave your money, leave your anything, no! I simply say leave your private worlds of dreams. That is *sannyas* for me. The old *sannyas* was leaving this world, the visible. One goes to the Himalayas, leaves the wife and children—that is not the point at all. That is not the world to leave, how can you leave it? Even the Himalayas belong to this world. The real world that has to be renounced is the mind, the private dreaming world. If you renounce it, then even sitting in the market you are in the Himalayas. If you don't renounce it, in the Himalayas also you will create a private world around you.

How can you escape yourself? Wherever you go, you will be with yourself. Wherever you go, you will behave in the same way. Situations may be different, but how can you be different? You will be asleep in the Himalayas. What difference does it make whether you sleep in Pune or in Boston, or you sleep in London or in the Himalayas? Wherever you are, you will be dreaming. Drop dreaming! Become more alert. Suddenly dreams disappear, and with dreams all miseries disappear.

> *Whatever we see when awake is death,*
> *when asleep, dreams.*

This is really beautiful. Whenever you are asleep, you see dreams, illusions, mirages—your own creation, your own private world. When you are awake, what do you see? Says Heraclitus, "When you are awake, you see death all around."

Maybe that's why you don't want to see. Maybe that's why you dream and create a cloud of dreams around you, so that you are not required to face the fact of death. But remember: a man becomes religious only when he encounters death, never before.

When you encounter death, when you see it face-to-face, when you don't avoid, when you don't dodge, when you don't escape, when you don't create a cloud around you—when you face it, encounter it, the fact of death—suddenly you become aware that death is life. The deeper you move into death, the deeper you move in life because, Heraclitus says, the opposites meet and mingle; they are one.

If you are trying to escape from death, remember, you will be escaping from life also. That's why you look so dead. This is the paradox: escape death and you remain dead; face, encounter death and you become alive. At the moment when you face death so deeply, so intensely that you start feeling that you are dying—not only around, but within also, you feel and touch death—the crisis comes. That is the cross of Jesus, the crisis of dying. At that moment, from one world you die—the world of the horizontal, the world of the mind—and you resurrect into another world.

Jesus' resurrection is not a physical phenomenon. Christians have been unnecessarily creating so many hypotheses around it. It is not a resurrection of this body, it is a resurrection into another dimension of this body; it is a resurrection into another dimension of another body that never dies. This body is temporal, that body is eternal. Jesus resurrects into another world, the world of the truth. The private world has disappeared.

In the last moment Jesus says he is worried, troubled. Even a man like Jesus dying is worried, it has to be so. He says to God, he cries, "What are you doing to me?" He would like to cling to the horizontal, he would like to cling to life—even a man like Jesus.

So don't feel guilty about yourself. You would also like to cling. This is the human in Jesus, and he is more human than Buddha, Mahavira. This is the human: the man comes to face death and he is troubled, and he cries, but he doesn't go back; he doesn't fall. Immediately he becomes aware of what he is asking. Then he says, "Thy will be done!"—relaxes, surrenders. Immediately the wheel turns—he is no longer in the horizontal; he has entered the vertical, the depth. There he is resurrected into eternity.

Die to time so that you are resurrected into eternity. Die to mind so you become alive in consciousness. Die to thinking so that you are born into awareness.

Says Heraclitus, "Whatever we see when awake is death." That's why we live in dreams, sleeps, tranquilizers, narcotics, intoxicants—in order not to face the fact. But the fact has to be faced. If you face it, the fact becomes the truth; if you escape, you live in lies. If you face the fact, the fact becomes the door for the truth. The fact is death; that has to be faced. And the truth will be life, eternal life, life in abundance, life that never ends.

AWARENESS AND CENTERING

First it must be understood what is meant by awareness. You are walking. You are aware of many things—of the shops, of people passing by you, of the traffic, of everything. You are aware of many things, only unaware of one thing—and that is yourself. You are walking on the street, you are aware of many things, and you are only not aware of yourself! This awareness of the self, George Gurdjieff has called self-remembering. Gurdjieff says, "Constantly, wherever you are, remember yourself."

Whatsoever you are doing, go on doing one thing inside continuously: be aware of yourself doing it. You are eating—be aware of yourself. You are walking—be aware of yourself. You are listening, you are speaking—be aware of yourself. When you are angry, be aware that you are angry. In the very moment that anger is there, be aware that you are angry. This constant remembering of the self creates a subtle energy, a very subtle energy in you. You begin to be a crystallized being.

Ordinarily, you are just a loose bag! No crystallization, no center really—just a liquidity, just a loose combination of many things without any center. A crowd, constantly shifting and changing, with no master inside. Awareness is what makes you a master—and when I say a master, I do not mean a controller. When I say be a master, I mean be a presence—a continuous presence. Whatever you are doing, or not doing, one thing must constantly be in your consciousness, that you *are*.

> Awareness is what makes you a master—and when I say a master, I do not mean a controller. When I say be a master, I mean be a presence—a continuous presence. Whatever you are doing, or not doing, one thing must constantly be in your consciousness, that you *are*.

This simple feeling of oneself, that one is, creates a center—a center of stillness, a center of silence, a center of inner mastery. It is an inner power. And when I say "an inner power," I mean it literally. That is why the buddhas talk about "the fire of awareness"—it *is* a fire. If you begin to be aware, you begin to feel a new energy in you, a new fire, a new life. And because of this new life, new power, new energy, many things that were dominating you just dissolve. You don't have to fight with them.

You have to fight with your anger, your greed, your sex, because you are weak. So really, anger, greed, and sex are not the problems, weakness is the problem. Once you begin to be stronger inside, with a feeling of inner presence—that you *are*—your energies become concentrated, crystallized on a single point, and a self is born. Remember, not an ego but a self is born. Ego is a false sense of self. Without having any self you go on believing that you have a self—that is ego. Ego means a false self—you are not a self, still you believe that you are a self.

Maulungputra, a seeker of truth, came to Buddha. Buddha asked him, "What are you seeking?"

Maulungputra said, "I am seeking my self. Help me!"

Buddha asked him to promise that he would do whatsoever was suggested. Maulungputra began to weep and said, "How can I promise? I am not—I am not yet, how can I promise? I do not know what I am going to be tomorrow; I do not have any self that can promise, so do not ask the impossible. I will try. I can say this much at the most—I will try. But I cannot say that whatsoever you say I will do, because who will do it? I am seeking that which can promise and can fulfill a promise. I am not yet."

Buddha said, "Maulungputra, I asked you that question to hear this. If you had promised, I would have turned you out. Had you said, 'I promise that I will do it,' then I would have known

> Ego is a false sense of self. Without having any self you go on believing that you have a self—that is ego.

that you are not really a seeker for the self, because a seeker must know that he is not yet. Otherwise, what is the purpose of seeking? If you are already, there is no need. You are not! And if one can feel this, then the ego evaporates."

Ego is a false notion of something that is not there at all. "Self" means a center that can promise. This center is created by being continuously aware, constantly aware. Be aware that you are doing something—that you are sitting, that now you are going to sleep, that now sleep is coming to you, that you are falling. Try to be conscious in every moment, and then you will begin to feel that a center is born within you; things have begun to crystallize, a centering is there. Everything now is related to a center.

We are without centers. Sometimes we feel centered, but those are moments when a situation makes you aware. If suddenly there is a situation, a dangerous situation, you will begin to feel a center in you because in danger you become aware. If someone is going to kill you, you cannot think in that moment; you cannot be unconscious in that moment. Your whole energy is centered, and that moment becomes solid. You cannot move to the past, you cannot move to the future—this very moment becomes everything. And then you are not only aware of the killer, you become aware of yourself, the one who is being killed. In that subtle moment you begin to feel a center in yourself.

That is why dangerous games have their appeal. Ask someone going to the top of Gourishankar, of Mount Everest. When for the first time Hillary was there he must have felt a sudden center. And when for the first time someone was on the moon, a sudden feeling of a center must have come. That is why danger has appeal. You are driving a car and you go on to greater and greater speed, and then the speed becomes dangerous. Then you cannot think; thoughts cease. Then you cannot dream. Then you cannot imagine. Then the present becomes solid. In that dangerous moment when at any instant death is possible, you are suddenly aware of a center in yourself. Danger has appeal only because in danger you sometimes feel centered.

Nietzsche somewhere says that war must continue because only in war is a self sometimes felt—a center is felt—because war is danger. And when death becomes a reality, life becomes intense. When death is just near, life becomes intense and you are centered. In any moment when you become aware of yourself there is a centering. But if it is situational, then when the situation is over, it will disappear.

It must not be just situational, it must be inner. So try to be aware in every ordinary activity. When sitting on your chair, try it— be aware of the sitter. Not only of the chair, not only of the room, of the surrounding atmosphere, be aware of the sitter. Close your eyes and feel yourself; dig deep and feel yourself.

Eugen Herrigel was learning with a Zen master. He was learning archery for three years. And the master would always say, "It is good. Whatsoever you are doing is good, but not enough." Herrigel himself became a master archer. His aim became 100 percent perfect, and still the master would say, "You are doing well, but it is not enough."

"With one hundred percent perfect aim!" said Herrigel. "Then what is your expectation? How can I now go further? With one hundred percent accuracy, how can you expect any more?"

The Zen master is reported to have said, "I am not concerned with your archery or your aim. I am concerned with you. You have become a perfect technician. But when your arrow leaves the bow, you are not aware of yourself, so it is futile! I am not concerned with the arrow reaching the target. I am concerned with you! When the arrow in the bow is arrowed, inside also your consciousness must be arrowed. Even if you miss the target, it makes no difference, but the inner target must not be missed, and you are missing that. You have become a perfect technician, but you are an imitator." But to a Western mind or, really, to a modern mind—and the Western mind is the modern mind—it is difficult to conceive of this. It appears nonsense. Archery is concerned with a particular efficiency of aiming.

By and by Herrigel became disappointed, and one day he said, "Now I am leaving. It seems impossible! It is impossible! When you are aiming at something, your awareness goes to your aim, to the object, and if you are to be a successful archer, you have to forget yourself—to remember only the aim, the target, and forget everything. Only the target must be there." But the Zen master was continually forcing Herrigel to create another target inside. This arrow must be double-arrowed: pointing toward the target outside and continuously pointing toward the inside—the self.

Herrigel said, "Now I will leave. It seems impossible. Your conditions cannot be fulfilled." And the day he was leaving, he was just sitting. He had come to take leave of the master, and the master was aiming at another target. Someone else was learning, and for the first time Herrigel was not involved. He had just come to take leave; he was sitting there. The moment the master was finished with his teaching, Herrigel would take his leave and go.

But then, suddenly, he became aware of the master and the double-arrowed consciousness of the master. The master was aiming. For three years continuously Herrigel had been with the same master, but he was more concerned with his own effort. He had never seen this man, what he was doing. For the first time he saw and realized— and suddenly, spontaneously, with no effort, he came to the master, took the bow from his hand, aimed at the target, and released the arrow. And the master said, "Okay! For the first time you have done it. I am happy."

What had he done? For the first time he was centered in himself. The target was there, but he was also there—present.

So whatsoever you are doing—whatsoever; no need of any archery—whatsoever you are doing, even just sitting, be double-arrowed. Remember what is going on outside and also remember who is inside.

Lin-chi was lecturing one morning and someone suddenly asked, "Just answer me one question: Who am I?" Lin-chi got down and went to the man. The whole hall became silent. What was he going to do? It was a simple question. He should have answered from his seat. He reached the man. The whole hall was silent. Lin-chi stood before the questioner looking into his eyes. It was a penetrating moment. Everything stopped. The questioner began to perspire. Lin-chi was just staring into his eyes. And then Lin-chi said, "Do not ask me. Go inside and find out who is asking. Close your eyes. Do not ask 'Who am I?' Go inside and find out who is asking, who is this questioner inside. Forget me. Find the source of the question. Go deep inside!"

> It is difficult to be aware even for a single moment; the mind is constantly flickering. But it is not impossible. It is arduous, it is difficult, but it is not impossible.

And it is reported that the man closed his eyes, became silent, and suddenly he was an enlightened one. He opened his eyes, laughed, touched the feet of Lin-chi, and said, "You have answered me. I have been asking everyone this question and many answers were given to me, but nothing proved to be an answer. But you have answered me."

"Who am I?" How can anyone answer it? But in that particular situation—a thousand persons silent, a pin-drop silence—Lin-chi came down with penetrating eyes and then just ordered the man, "Close your eyes, go inside, and find out who the questioner is. Do not wait for me to answer. Find out who has asked." And the man closed his eyes. What happened in that situation? He became centered. Suddenly he was centered, suddenly he became aware of the innermost core.

This has to be discovered, and awareness means the method to discover this innermost core. The more unconscious you are, the further away you are from yourself. The more conscious, the nearer you reach to yourself. If the consciousness is total, you are at the center. If the consciousness is less, you are near the periphery. When you are unconscious, you are on the periphery where the center is completely forgotten. So these are the two possible ways to move.

You can move to the periphery—then you move to unconsciousness. Sitting at a film, sitting somewhere listening to music, you can forget yourself—then you are on the periphery. Reading the Bhagavad Gita or the Bible or the Koran, you can forget yourself—then you are on the periphery.

Whatsoever you do, if you can remember yourself, then you are nearer to the center. Then someday suddenly you are centered. Then you have energy. That energy is the fire. The whole of life, the whole of existence, is energy, is fire. *Fire* is the old name; now they call it electricity. Man has been labeling it with many, many names, but *fire* is good. *Electricity* seems a little bit dead; *fire* looks more alive.

Act mindfully. It is a long, arduous journey, and it is difficult to be aware even for a single moment; the mind is

> Awareness is the technique for centering oneself, for achieving the inner fire. It is there, hidden, it can be discovered.

constantly flickering. But it is not impossible. It is arduous, it is difficult, but it is not impossible. It is possible—for everyone it is possible. Only effort is needed, and a wholehearted effort. Nothing should be left out; nothing should be left inside untouched. Everything should be sacrificed for awareness; only then is the inner flame discovered. It is there.

If one goes to find out the essential unity among all the religions that have existed or that may ever exist, then this single word *awareness* can be found.

Jesus tells a story. . . . A master of a big house has gone out, and he has told his servants to be constantly alert, because any moment he can come back. So for twenty-four hours a day they have to be alert. Any moment the master can come—any moment! There is no fixed moment, no fixed day, no fixed date. If there is a fixed date, then you can sleep; then you can do whatsoever you like and be alert only on that particular date because then the master is coming. But the master has said, "I will come at any moment. Day and night you have to be alert to receive me."

This is a parable of life. You cannot postpone; any moment the master may come. One has to be alert continuously. No date is fixed; nothing is known about when that sudden happening will be there. One can do only one thing: be alert and wait.

Awareness is the technique for centering oneself, for achieving the inner fire. It is there, hidden; it can be discovered. And once it is discovered,

> Your failures will be helpful. They can show you how unconscious you are. And even if you can become aware that you are unconscious, you have gained a certain awareness. If a madman becomes aware that he is mad, he is on the path toward sanity.

then only are we capable of entering the temple—not before, never before.

But we can deceive ourselves by symbols. Symbols are to show deeper realities to us, but we can use them as deceptions. We can burn incense, we can worship with outer things, and then we feel at ease that we have done something. We can feel ourselves religious without becoming religious at all. That is what is happening; that is what the earth has become. People think they are religious just because they are following outer symbols, with no inner fire.

Make efforts even if you are a failure. You will be in the beginning. You will fail again and again, but even your failure will help. When you fail to be aware for a single moment, you feel for the first time how unconscious you are.

Walk down the street, and you cannot walk a few steps without becoming unconscious. Again and again you forget yourself. You begin to read a signboard, and you forget yourself. Someone passes, you look at him, then you forget yourself.

Your failures will be helpful. They can show you how unconscious you are. And even if you can become aware that you are unconscious, you have gained a certain awareness. If a madman becomes aware that he is mad, he is on the path toward sanity.

MANY ILLNESSES, ONE PRESCRIPTION

You have tried not to be angry, you have decided so many times, but still it happens. You have tried not to be greedy, but again and again you fall in the trap. You have tried all kinds of things to change yourself, but nothing seems ever to happen. You remain the same.

And here I am saying that there is a simple key—awareness. You cannot believe it. How can awareness, just awareness, help when nothing else has been of any help? Keys are always very small; keys are not big things. A small key can open a big lock.

When people would ask Buddha, "What should we do not to be angry, or what should we do not to be greedy, or what should we do not to be so much obsessed with sex or food?" his answer was always the same: be aware. Bring awareness to your life.

His disciple Ananda, listening again and again to every kind of person—different problems, but the prescription of the physician remains the same—became puzzled. He said, "What is the matter with you? They bring different kinds of illness—somebody brings greed and somebody sex and somebody food and somebody something else—but your prescription remains the same!"

And Buddha said, "Their illnesses are different—just as people can dream different dreams."

If two thousand persons fall asleep, they will have two thousand dreams. But if you come to me and ask how to get rid of this dream, the medicine will remain the same: wake up! It is not going to be different; the prescription is going to be the same. You can call it awareness, you can call it witnessing, you can call it remembering, you can call it meditation—these are different names for the same medicine.

THE ANALYST AND THE WITNESS

The Western approach is to think about a problem, to find the causes of the problem, to go into the history of the problem, into the past of the problem, to uproot the problem from the very beginning. To uncondition the mind, or to recondition the mind, to recondition the body, to take out all those imprints that have been left on the brain—this is the Western approach. Psychoanalysis goes into the memory; it works there. It goes into your childhood, into your past; it moves backward. It finds out from where a problem has arisen—maybe fifty years before, when you were a child the problem arose in your relationship with your mother, then psychoanalysis will go back.

Fifty years of history! It is a long, dragging affair. And even then it doesn't help much because there are millions of problems; it is not only a question of one problem. You can go into one problem's history; you can look into your autobiography and find out the causes. Maybe you can eliminate one problem, but there are millions of problems. If you start going into each problem to solve one life's problems, you will need millions of lives! Let me repeat it: to solve one life's problems you will have to be born again and again, millions of times. This is almost impractical. This cannot be done. And all those millions of lives when you will be solving the problems of this life, those lives will create their own problems . . . and so on and so forth. You will be dragged more and more into the problems. This is absurd!

Now, the same psychoanalytical approach has gone toward the body: Rolfing, bioenergetics, and other methods try to eliminate imprints on the body, in the musculature. Again, you have to go into the history of the body. But one thing is certain about both the approaches, which work on the same logical pattern—that the problem comes from the past, so somehow it has to be tackled in the past.

Man's mind has always been trying to do two impossible things. One is to reform the past—which cannot be done. The past has happened. You cannot really go into the past. When you think of going into the past, at the most you go into the memory of it; it is not the real past, it is just the memory. The past is no more, so you cannot reform it. This is one of the impossible goals of humanity, and man has suffered very much because of it. You want to undo the past—how can you undo it? The past is absolute. The past means that all the potential of a thing is finished; it has become actual. Now there is no longer any potential to reform it, to undo it, to redo it. You cannot do anything with the past.

And the second impossible idea that has always dominated the human mind is to establish the future—which again, cannot be done. Future means that which is not yet; you cannot establish it. Future remains unestablished, future remains open.

Future is pure potentiality; unless it happens, you cannot be certain about it. Past is pure actuality; it has happened. Now nothing can be done about it. Between these two, man stands in the present always thinking of the impossibles. He wants to make everything certain about the future, about tomorrow—which cannot be done. Let it sink as deeply in your heart

> You want to undo the past—how can you undo it? The past is absolute. The past means that all the potential of a thing is finished, it has become actual. Now there is no longer any potential to reform it, to undo it, to redo it.

as possible: *it cannot be done.* Don't waste your present moment trying to make the future certain. The future is uncertainty; that is the very quality of the future. And don't waste your time looking back. The past has happened, it is a dead phenomenon. Nothing can be done about it. At the most what you can do is reinterpret it, that's all. That's what psychoanalysis is doing: reinterpreting it. Reinterpretation can be done, but the past remains the same.

Psychoanalysis and astrology—astrology tries somehow to make the future certain, and psychoanalysis tries to redo the past. Neither is a science. Both things are impossible, but both have millions of followers—because man likes it that way! He wants to be certain about the future, so he goes to the astrologer, he consults the I Ching, he goes to a tarot reader, and there are a thousand and one ways to fool oneself, to deceive oneself. And then there are

> Future is pure potentiality, unless it happens, you cannot be certain about it. Past is pure actuality, it has happened. Now nothing can be done about it. Between these two, man stands in the present always thinking of the impossibles.

people who say they can change the past—he consults them also.

Once these two things are dropped, you become free of all sorts of foolishnesses. Then you don't go to the psychoanalyst and you don't go to the astrologer. Then you know the past is finished—you will also be finished with it. And the future has not happened. Whenever it happens, we will see—nothing can be done about it right now. You can only destroy the present moment, which is the only moment available, real.

The West has continuously been looking into problems, how to solve them. The West takes problems seriously. And when you are going in a certain logic, given the premises, that logic looks perfect.

I was just reading one anecdote:

A great philosopher and world-renowned mathematician is aboard an airplane. He is sitting in his seat and thinking about great mathematical problems, when suddenly an announcement comes from the captain: "I am sorry, there will be a slight delay. Engine number one has cut out and we are now flying on three engines."

About ten minutes later another announcement: "I am afraid there will be further delay—engines two and three have cut out and there is only number four left."

So the philosopher turns to the fellow sitting next to him and says, "Good golly! If the other one cuts out, we will be up here all night!"

When you are thinking along a certain line, the very direction of it makes certain things possible—absurd things also possible. Once you have taken human problems seriously, once you start thinking about man as a problem, you have accepted some premise, you have taken the first step wrongly. Now you can go in that direction, and you can go on and on. Now such a great amount of literature has developed about mind phenomena, psychoanalysis; millions of papers are written, and treatises and books. Once Freud opened the doors of a certain logic, it dominated the whole century.

The East has a totally different outlook. First, it says no problem is serious. The moment you say no problem is serious, the problem is almost 99 percent

> The moment you say no problem is serious, the problem is almost 99 percent dead. Your whole vision changes about it.

dead. Your whole vision changes about it. The second thing the East says is that the problem is there because you are *identified* with it. It has nothing to do with the past, nothing to do with its history. You are identified with it—that is the real thing. And that is the key to solving all problems.

For example, you are an angry person. If you go to the psycho-analyst, he will say, "Go into the past . . . how did this anger arise? In what situations did it become more and more conditioned and imprinted on your mind? We will have to wash out all those imprints; we will have to wipe them off. We will have to clean your past completely."

If you go to an Eastern mystic, he will say, "You think that you *are* anger, you feel identified with the anger—that is where things are going wrong. Next time anger happens, you just be a watcher, you just be a witness. Don't get identified with the anger. Don't say, 'I am anger.' Don't say, 'I am angry.' Just see it happening as if it is happening on a TV screen. Look at yourself as if you are looking at somebody else."

You are pure consciousness. When the cloud of anger comes around you, just watch it—and remain alert so that you don't get identified. The whole thing is how not to become identified with the problem. Once you have learned it . . . then there is no question of having "so many problems"—because the key, the same key will open all the locks. It is so with anger, it is so with greed, it is so with sex. It is so with everything else that the mind is capable of.

The East says, just remain uniden-

> The whole thing is how not to become identified with the problem. Once you have learned it . . . then there is no question of having "so many problems"— because the key, the same key will open all the locks.

tified. Remember—that's what George Gurdjieff means when he talks about "self-remembering." Remember that you are a witness, be mindful—that's what Buddha says. Be alert that a cloud is passing by—maybe the cloud comes from the past, but that is meaningless. It must have a certain past, it cannot come just out of the blue. It must be coming from a certain sequence of events—but that is irrelevant. Why be bothered about it? Right now, this very moment, you can become detached from it. You can cut yourself away from it, the bridge can be broken right now—and it can be broken *only* in the now.

Going into the past won't help. Thirty years before, the anger arose and you got identified with it that day. Now, you cannot get unidentified from that past—it is no longer there! But you can get unidentified *this* moment, this very moment—and then the whole series of angers of your past is no more part of you. You will not have to go back and undo whatsoever your parents and your society and the priest and the church have done—that will be a sheer waste of precious present time. In the first place it has destroyed many years; now, again, it will be destroying your present moments. You can simply drop out of it, just as a snake slips out of the old skin.

The past and its conditionings do exist—but they exist either in the body or in the brain; they don't exist in your consciousness because the consciousness cannot be conditioned. Consciousness remains free—freedom is its innermost quality, freedom is its nature.

> The past and its conditionings do exist— but they exist either in the body or in the brain, they don't exist in your consciousness because the consciousness cannot be conditioned. Consciousness remains free—freedom is its innermost quality, freedom is its nature.

You can look—so many years of repression, so many years of a certain education. In this moment when you are looking at it, this consciousness is no longer identified; otherwise, who will be aware? If you had really *become* repressed, then who would be aware? Then there would be no possibility of becoming aware.

If you can say "I spent twenty-one years in a crazy educational system," one thing is certain: you are not yet crazy. The system has failed; it didn't work. You are not crazy, hence you can see the whole system as crazy. A madman cannot see that he is mad. Only a sane person can see that this is madness. To see madness as madness, sanity is needed. Those twenty-one years of crazy system have failed; all that repressive conditioning has failed. It cannot really succeed—it succeeds only in the proportion that you get identified with it. Any moment you can stand aloof . . . it is there, I am not saying it is not there: but it is no longer part of your consciousness.

This is the beauty of consciousness—consciousness can slip out of anything. There is no barrier to it, no boundary to it. Just a moment before you were an Englishman—understanding the nonsense of nationalism, a second later you are no longer an Englishman. I am not saying that your white skin will change; it will remain white—but you are no longer identified with the whiteness; you are no longer against the black. You see the stupidity of it. I am not saying that just by seeing that you are no longer an Englishman you will forget the English language, no. It will still be there in your memory, but your consciousness has slipped out, your consciousness is standing on a hill looking at the valley—now, the Englishman is dead in the valley and you are standing on the hills, far away, unattached, untouched.

The whole Eastern methodology can be reduced to one word: witnessing. And the whole Western methodology can be reduced to one thing: analyzing. Analyzing, you go round and round. Witnessing, you simply get out of the circle.

Analysis is a vicious circle. If you really go into analysis, you will simply be puzzled—how is it possible? If, for example, you try to go

> ☙
>
> The whole Eastern methodology can be reduced to one word: witnessing. And the whole Western methodology can be reduced to one thing: analyzing. Analyzing, you go round and round. Witnessing, you simply get out of the circle.

into the past, where will you end? Where exactly? If you go into the past, where did your sexuality start? When you were fourteen years of age? But then it came out of the blue? It must have been getting ready in the body, so when? When you were born? But then when you were in the mother's womb, wasn't it getting ready? Then when, the moment you were conceived? But before that, half of your sexuality was mature in your mother's egg and half of the sexuality was maturing in your father's sperm. Now go on . . . where will you end? You will have to go to Adam and Eve! And even then it does not end: you will have to go to Father God Himself—why in the first place did he create Adam? . . .

Analysis will always remain half, so analysis never helps anybody really. It cannot help. It makes you a little more adjusted to your reality, that's all. It is a sort of adjustment, it helps you to attain a little bit of understanding about your problems, their genesis, how they have arisen. And that little intellectual understanding helps you to adjust to the society better, but you remain the same person. There is no transformation through it, there is no radical change through it.

Witnessing is a revolution. It is a radical change from the very roots. It brings a totally new human being into existence, because it takes your consciousness out of all the conditionings. Conditionings are there in the body and in the mind, but consciousness remains unconditioned. It is pure, always pure. It is virgin; its virginity cannot be violated.

The Eastern approach is to make you mindful of this virgin consciousness, of this purity, of this innocence. The Eastern emphasis is on the sky, and the Western emphasis is on the clouds. Clouds have a genesis; if you find out from where they come, you will have to go to the ocean, then to the sun rays and the evaporation of the water, and the clouds forming . . . and you can go on, but it will be moving in a circle. The clouds form, then again they come, fall in love with the trees, start pouring again into the earth, become rivers, go to the ocean, start evaporating, rising again on sun rays, become clouds, again fall on the earth . . . It goes on and on, round and round and round. It is a wheel. From where will you come out? One thing will lead to another and you will be in the wheel.

The sky has no genesis. The sky is uncreated; it is not produced by anything. In fact, for anything to be, a sky is needed as a must, a priori; it has to exist before anything else can exist. You can ask the Christian theologian—he says, "God created the world." Ask him whether before God created the world there was any sky or not. If there was no sky, where did God used to exist? He must have needed space. If there was no space, where did he create the world? Where did he put the world? Space is a must, even for God to exist. You cannot say, "God created space." That would be absurd, because then he would not have had any space to exist. Space must precede God.

> Analysis never helps anybody really. It is a sort of adjustment, it helps you to attain a little bit of understanding about your problems, and that little intellectual understanding helps you to adjust to the society better, but you remain the same person. There is no transformation through it.

The sky has always been there. The Eastern approach is to become mindful of the sky. The Western approach makes you more and more alert to the clouds and helps you a little, but it doesn't make you aware of your innermost core. Circumference, yes, you become a little more aware of the circumference, but not aware of the center. And the circumference is a cyclone.

You have to find the center of the cyclone. And that happens only through witnessing.

Witnessing will not change your conditioning. Witnessing will not change your body musculature. But witnessing will give you an experience that you are beyond all musculature, all conditioning. In that moment of beyondness, in that moment of transcendence, no problem exists—not for you.

And now it is up to you. The body will still carry the musculature, and the mind will still carry the conditioning—now it is up to you. If sometimes you are hankering for the problem, you can get into the bodymind and have the problem and enjoy it. If you don't want to have it, you can remain out. The problem will remain as an imprint in the bodymind phenomenon, but you will be aloof and away from it.

That's how a buddha functions. You use memory, a buddha also uses memory—but he is not identified with it. He uses memory as a mechanism. For example, I am using language. When I have to use language, I use the

> Witnessing will not change your conditioning. Witnessing will not change your body musculature. But witnessing will give you an experience that you are beyond all musculature, all conditioning. In that moment of beyondness, in that moment of transcendence, no problem exists.

mind and all the imprints, but as a continuum, I am not the mind; that awareness is there. So I remain the boss, the mind remains a servant. When the mind is called, it comes; its utility is there—but it cannot dominate.

So problems will exist, but they will exist only in the seed form in the body and the mind. How can you change your past? You have been a Catholic in the past; if for forty years you have been a Catholic, how can you change those forty years and not be a Catholic? No, those forty years will remain as a period of being Catholic—but you can slip out of it. Now you know that that was just identification. Those forty years cannot be destroyed, and there is no need to destroy them. If you are the master of the house, there is no need. You can use even those forty years in a certain way, in a creative way. Even that crazy education can be used in a creative way.

> If you feel too lonely and you want problems, you can have them. If you feel too miserable without misery, you can have them. They will remain always available, but there is no need to have them, there is no necessity to have them. It will be your choice.

All the imprints left on the brain, on the musculature of the body . . . they will be there, but as a seed—*potentially* there. If you feel too lonely and you want problems, you can have them. If you feel too miserable without misery, you can have them. They will remain always available, but there is no need to have them, there is no necessity to have them. It will be your choice.

WITNESSING IS THE TECHNIQUE FOR CENTERING. We have discussed centering—a man can live in two ways: he can live from his periphery or he can live from his center. The periphery belongs to the ego and the center belongs to the being. If you live from the ego, you are always related with the other. The periphery is related with the other.

Whatsoever you do is not an action, it is always a reaction—you do it in response to something done to you. From the periphery there is no action, everything is a reaction—nothing comes from your center. In a way, you are just a slave of the circumstances. You are not doing anything; rather, you are being forced.

From the center, the situation changes diametrically. From the center you begin to act; for the first time you begin to exist not as a *relata* but in your own right.

Buddha is passing through a village. Some people are angry, very much against his teachings. They abuse him, they insult him. Buddha listens silently and then says, "If you are finished, then allow me to move on. I have to reach the next village, and they will be waiting for me. If something is still remaining in your mind, then when I am passing back by this route, you can finish it."

They say, "We have abused you, insulted you. Are you not going to answer?"

Buddha says, "I never react now. What you do is up to you—I never react now, you cannot force me to do something. You can abuse me; that is up to you—I am not a slave. I have become a free man. I act from my center, not from my periphery, and your abuse can touch only the periphery, not my center. My center remains untouched."

You are touched not because your center is touched, but only because you have no center. You are just the periphery, identified with the periphery. The periphery is bound to be touched by everything—everything that happens. It is just your boundary, so whatsoever happens is bound to touch it, and you don't have any center. The moment you have a center, then you have a distance from yourself—you have a distance from your periphery. Someone can abuse the periphery, but not you. You can remain aloof, detached—there is a distance between you and yourself. Between you as your periphery, and you as the center, there is a distance. And that distance cannot be broken by anyone else, because no one can penetrate to the center. The outside world can touch you only on the periphery.

So Buddha says, "Now I am centered. Ten years before it would have been different; if you had abused me, then I would have reacted. But now I only *act.*"

Understand clearly the distinction between reaction and action. You love someone because someone loves you.

> The moment you have a center, then you have a distance from yourself—you have a distance from your periphery. Someone can abuse the periphery, but not you. You can remain aloof, detached.

Buddha also loves you, not because you love him; that is irrelevant. Whether you love him or hate him is irrelevant—he loves you because it is an *act,* not a reaction. The act comes from you, and the reaction is forced upon you. Centering means now you have begun to act.

Another point to be remembered: when you act, the act is always total. When you react, it can never be total. It is always partial, fragmentary, because when I act from my periphery—that is, when I *react*—it cannot be total because I am not involved in it, really. Only my periphery is involved, so it cannot be total. So if you love from your periphery, your love can never be total—it is always partial. And that means much, because if love is partial, then the remaining space will be filled by hate. If your kindness is partial, the remaining space will be filled by cruelty. If your goodness is partial, then who will fill the remaining space? If your God is partial, then you will need a devil to fill the remaining space.

That means a partial act is bound to be contradictory, in conflict with itself. Modern psychology says you both love and hate simultaneously. Amphibian is your mind, contradictory—to the same object you are related with love and with hate. And if love and hate are both there, then there is going to be confusion—and a poisonous confusion. Your kindness is mixed with cruelty and your charity is theft and your prayer becomes a kind of violence. Even if you try to be a saint on the periphery, your sainthood is bound to be tinged with sin. On the periphery, everything is going to be self-contradictory.

Only when you act from the center is your act total. And when that act is total, it has a beauty of its own. When the act is total, it is moment to moment. When the act is total, you don't carry the memory—you need not! When the act is partial, it is a suspended thing.

You eat something—if the eating is partial, then when the actual eating is finished, you will continue eating in the mind. It will remain suspended. Only a total thing can have an end and can have a beginning. A partial thing is just a continuous series with no beginning and with no end. You are in your home, and you have carried your shop and the marketplace with you. You are in your shop, and you have carried your house and household affairs. You are never—you can never be—at any single moment totally in it, so much is being carried continuously. This is the heaviness, the tense heaviness on the mind, on the heart.

A total act has a beginning and an

> Only when you act from the center is your act total. And when that act is total, it has a beauty of its own. When the act is total, it is moment to moment. When the act is total, you don't carry the memory—you need not.

74

end. It is atomic; it is not a series. It is there and then it is not there. You are completely free from it to move into the unknown. Otherwise one goes on in grooves, the mind becomes just grooved. You go on moving in the same circular way, in a vicious circle. Because the past is never finished, it comes into the present. It goes on and penetrates into the future.

So, really, a partial mind, a peripheral mind, carries its past—and the past is a big thing! Even if you don't consider past lives, even then, the past is a big thing. Fifty years' experiences, beautiful and ugly, but unfinished—everything unfinished, so you go on carrying a fifty-year-long past that is dead. This dead past will fall upon a single moment of the present—it is bound to kill it!

So you cannot live, it is impossible. With this past upon you, you cannot live—every single moment is so fresh and so delicate, this whole dead weight will kill it. It is killing! Your past goes on killing your present, and when the present is dead, it becomes a part of the burden. When it is alive, it is not part of you—when it becomes dead, when it has been killed by your dead past, then it becomes yours, then it is part of you. This is the situation.

The moment you begin to act from the center, every act is total, atomic. It is there and then it is not there. You are completely free from it. Then you can move with no burden—unburdened. And only then can you live in the new moment that is always there, by coming to it fresh. But you can come to it fresh only when there is no past to be carried.

And you will have to carry the past if it is unfinished—the mind has a tendency to finish everything. If it is unfinished, then it has to be carried. If something has remained unfinished during the day, then you will dream about it in the night, because the mind tends to finish everything. The moment it is finished, the mind is unburdened from it. Unless it is finished, the mind is bound to come to it again and again.

Whatsoever you are doing—your love, your sex, your friendship—everything is unfinished. And you cannot make it total if you remain on the periphery. So how to be centered in oneself? How to

> If something has remained unfinished during the day, then you will dream about it in the night, because the mind tends to finish everything. The moment it is finished, the mind is unburdened from it. Unless it is finished, the mind is bound to come to it again and again.

attain this centering so that you are not on the periphery? Witnessing is the technique.

This word *witnessing* is a most significant word. There are hundreds of techniques to achieve centering, but witnessing is bound to be a part, a basic part, in every technique. Whatsoever the technique may be, witnessing will be the essential part in it. So it will be better to call it the technique of all techniques. It is not simply a technique; the process of witnessing is the essential part of *all* the techniques.

One can talk about witnessing as a pure technique, also. For example, J. Krishnamurti—he is talking about witnessing as a pure technique. But that talk is just like talking about the spirit without the body. You cannot feel it, you cannot see it. Everywhere the spirit is embodied—you can feel the spirit *through* the body. Of course the spirit is not the body, but you can feel it through the body. Every technique is just a body, and witnessing is the soul. You can talk about witnessing independent of any body, any matter; then it becomes abstract, totally abstract. So Krishnamurti has been talking continuously for half a century, but whatsoever he is saying is so pure, unembodied, that one thinks that one is understanding but that understanding remains just a concept.

In this world nothing exists as pure spirit. Everything exists embodied. Witnessing is the spirit of all spiritual techniques, and all the techniques are bodies, different bodies.

So first we must understand what witnessing is, and then we can understand witnessing through some bodies, some techniques.

We know thinking, and one has to start from thinking to know what witnessing means because one has to start from what one knows. We know thinking—thinking means judgment; you see something and you judge. You see a flower and you say it is beautiful or not beautiful. You hear a song and you appreciate it or you don't appreciate it. You appreciate something or you condemn something. Thinking is judgment—the moment you think, you have begun to judge.

Thinking is evaluation. You cannot think without evaluation. How can you think about a flower without evaluating it? The moment you start thinking, you will say it is beautiful or not beautiful. You will have to use some category because thinking is categorizing. The moment you have categorized a thing—labeled it, named it— you have thought about it.

Thinking is impossible if you are not going to judge. If you are not going to judge, then you can just remain aware—but you cannot think.

A flower is here, and I say to you, "See it, but don't think. Look at the flower but don't think." So what can you do? If thinking is not allowed, what can you do? You can only witness; you can only be aware. You can only be conscious of the flower. You can face the fact—the flower is here. Now you can encounter it. If thinking is not allowed, you cannot say, "It is beautiful. It is not beautiful. I know about it," or, "It is strange—I have never seen it." You cannot say anything. Words cannot be used because every word has a value in it. Every word is a judgment. Language is burdened with judgment; language can never be impartial. The moment you use a word, you have judged.

So you cannot use language, you cannot verbalize. If I say, "This

> ⌐
>
> Thinking is impossible
> if you are not going
> to judge. If you are
> not going to judge,
> then you can just
> remain aware—but
> you cannot think.

is a flower—look at it, but don't think," then verbalization is not allowed. So what can you do? You can only be a witness. If you are there without thinking, just facing something, it is witnessing. Then witnessing means a passive awareness. Remember—passive. Thinking is active, you are doing something. Whatsoever you are seeing, you are doing something with it. You are not just passive, you are not like a mirror—you are doing something. And the moment you do something, you have changed the thing.

I see a flower and I say, "It is beautiful!"—I have changed it. Now I have imposed something on the flower. Now, whatsoever the flower is, to me it is a flower plus my feeling of its being beautiful. Now the flower is far away; in between the flower and me is my sense of judgment, my evaluation of its being beautiful. Now the flower is not the same to me, the quality has changed. I have come into it—now my judgment has penetrated into the fact. Now it is more like a fiction and less like a fact.

This feeling that the flower is beautiful doesn't belong to the flower, it belongs to me. I have entered the fact. Now the fact is not virgin, I have corrupted it. Now my mind has become part of it. Really, to say that my mind has become part of it means that my past has become part of it, because when I say, "This flower is beautiful," it means I have judged it through my past knowledge. How can you say that this flower is beautiful? Your experiences of the past, your conceptions of the past, that something like this is beautiful—you have judged it according to your past.

Mind means your past, your memories. The past has come upon the present. You have destroyed a virgin fact; now it is distorted. Now there is no flower—the flower as a reality in itself is no longer there. It is corrupted by you, destroyed by you; your past has come in between. You have interpreted—this is thinking. Thinking means bringing the past to a present fact.

That's why thinking can never lead you to the truth—because truth is virgin and has to be faced in its total virginity. The moment you bring your past in, you are destroying it. Then it is an interpretation, not a realization of the fact. You have disrupted it; the purity is lost.

Thinking means bringing your past to the present. Witnessing means no past, just the present—no bringing in of the past.

> Thinking means bringing your past to the present. Witnessing means no past, just the present— no bringing in of the past.

Witnessing is passive. You are not doing anything—you are! Simply, you are there. Only you are present. The flower is present, you are present— then there is a relationship of witnessing. When the flower is present and your whole past is present, not you, then it is a relationship of thinking.

So start from thinking. What is thinking? It is the bringing of the mind into the present. You have missed the present then—you have missed it totally! The moment the past penetrates into the present, you have missed it. When you say, "This flower is beautiful," really it has become the past. When you say, "This flower is beautiful," it is a past experience. You have known, you have judged.

When the flower is there and you are there, even to say that this flower is beautiful is not possible. You cannot assert any judgment in the present. Any judgment, any assertion, belongs to the past. If I say, "I love you," it has become a thing that is past. If I say, "This flower is beautiful," I have felt, I have judged—it has become the past.

Witnessing is always present, never the past. Thinking is always the past. Thinking is dead, witnessing is alive. So the next distinction . . . First, thinking is active, doing something. Witnessing is passive, nondoing, just being. Thinking is always the past, the dead, which has gone away, which is no more. Witnessing is always the present—that which is.

So if you go on thinking, you can never know what witnessing is. To stop, to end thinking, becomes a start in witnessing. Cessation of thinking is witnessing.

So what to do?—because thinking is a long habit with us. It has become just a robotlike, mechanical thing. It is not that you think; it is not your decision now, it is a mechanical habit—you cannot do anything else. The moment a flower is there, the thinking has started. We have no nonverbal experiences; only small children have. Nonverbal experience is *really* experience. Verbalization is escaping from the experience.

When I say, "The flower is beautiful," the flower has vanished from me. Now it is my mind, not the flower, I am concerned with. Now it is the image of the flower in my mind, not the flower itself. Now the flower itself is a picture in the mind, a thought in the mind, and now I can compare with my past experiences and judge. But the flower is no more there.

When you verbalize, you are closed to experience. When you are nonverbally aware, you are open, vulnerable. Witnessing means a constant opening to experience, no closing.

What to do? This mechanical habit of so-called thinking has to be broken somewhere. So whatsoever you are doing, try to do it nonverbally. It is difficult, arduous, and in the beginning it seems absolutely impossible, but it is not. It is not impossible—it is difficult. You are walking on the street—walk nonverbally. Just walk, even if just for a few seconds, and you will have a glimpse of a different world—a nonverbal world, the real world, not the world of the mind man has created in himself.

You are eating—eat nonverbally. Someone asked Bokuju—Bokuju was a great Zen master—"What's your path, what's your way?"

So Bokuju said, "My path is very simple: when I am hungry, I eat; when I am sleepy, I sleep—and this is all."

The man was bewildered. He said, "What are you saying? I also eat and I also sleep, and everyone is doing the same. So what is in that that you call it a path?"

Bokuju said, "When you are eating, you are doing many things, not only eating. And when you are sleeping, you are doing everything else except sleeping. But when I eat, I simply eat; when I sleep, I simply sleep. Every act is total."

Every act becomes total if you are nonverbal. So try to eat without any verbalization in the mind, with no thinking in the mind. Just eat, and then eating becomes meditation—because if you are nonverbal, you will become a witness.

If you are verbal, you will become a thinker. If you are nonverbal, you cannot do anything about it, you cannot help it—you will be a witness, automatically. So try to do anything nonverbally: walk, eat, take a bath, or just sit silently. Then just sit—then *be* "a sitting." Don't think. Then even just sitting can become meditation; just walking can become meditation.

Someone else asked Bokuju, "Give me some technique of meditation."

Bokuju said, "I can give you a technique, but you will not be able to meditate—because you can practice a technique with a verbalizing mind." Your fingers can move on a rosary and you can go on thinking. If your fingers just move on the rosary with no thinking, it becomes a meditation. Then, really, no technique is needed. The whole of life is a technique. So Bokuju said, "It would be better if you can be with me and watch me. Don't ask for a method, just watch me and you will come to know."

The poor fellow watched for seven days. He began to be more confused. After seven days he said, "When I came, I was less confused. Now I am more confused. I have watched you for seven days continuously—what is there to be watched?"

Bokuju said, "Then you have not watched. When I walk, have

you seen?—I simply walk. When you bring tea in the morning for me, have you watched?—I simply take the tea and drink it—just drinking. There is no Bokuju—just drinking. No Bokuju—just drinking of the tea. Have you watched? If you have watched, then you must have felt that Bokuju is no more."

This is a subtle point—because if the thinker is there, then there is ego; then you are a Bokuju or somebody else. But if only action is there with no verbalization, no thinking, there is no ego. So Bokuju says, "Have you really watched? Then there was no Bokuju—just drinking of the tea, walking in the garden, digging a hole in the earth."

Buddha, because of this, has said there is no soul. Because you have not watched, you go on continuously thinking that you have a soul. You are not! If you are a witness, then you are not. The "I" forms itself through thoughts.

So one thing more: accumulated thoughts, piled-up memories, create the feeling of ego, that you *are*.

Try this experiment: cut your whole past away from you—no memory. You don't know who your parents are, you don't know to whom you belong—to which country, to which religion, to which race. You don't know where you were educated, whether you were educated or not. Just cut the whole past—and remember who you are.

You cannot remember who you are! You are, obviously. You are, but who are you? In this moment, you cannot feel an "I."

The ego is just accumulated past. The ego is your thought condensed, crystallized.

So Bokuju says, "If you have watched me, I was not. There was drinking of the tea, but no drinker. Walking was there in the garden, but no walker. Action was there, but no actor."

In witnessing, there is no sense of "I"—in thinking there is. So if the so-called thinkers are so deeply rooted in their egos, it is not just a coincidence. Artists, thinkers, philosophers, literary persons—if they are so egoistic, it is not just a coincidence. The more thoughts you have, the greater the ego you have.

In witnessing there is no ego—but this comes only if you can transcend language. Language is the barrier. Language is needed to communicate with others; it is not needed to communicate with oneself. It is a useful instrument—rather, the most useful instrument. Man could create a society, a world, only because of language. But because of language, man has forgotten himself.

Language is our world. If for a single moment man forgets his language, then what remains? Culture, society, Hinduism, Christianity, communism—what remains? Nothing remains. If only language is taken out of existence, the whole humanity with its culture, civilization, science, religion, philosophy, disappears.

Language is a communication with others; it is the only communication. It is useful, but it is dangerous—and whenever some instrument is useful, it is in the same proportion dangerous also. The danger is this, that the more mind moves into language, the farther away it goes from the center. So one needs a subtle balance and a subtle mastery to be capable of moving into language and also capable of leaving language, of moving out of language.

Witnessing means moving out of language, verbalization, mind.

Witnessing means a state of no-mind, no-thinking.

So try it! It is a long effort, and nothing is predictable—but try, and the effort will give you some moments when suddenly language disappears. And then a new dimension opens. You

> Language is needed to communicate with others; it is not needed to communicate with oneself. It is a useful instrument—rather, the most useful instrument. Man could create a society, a world, only because of language. But because of language, man has forgotten himself.

become aware of a different world—the world of simultaneity, the world of here and now, the world of no-mind, the world of reality.

Language must evaporate. So try to do ordinary acts, bodily movements, without language. Buddha used this technique to watch the breath. He would say to his disciples, "Go on watching your breath. Don't do anything: just watch the breath coming in, the breath going out, the breath coming in, the breath going out." It is not to be said like this, it is to be felt—the breath coming in, with no words. Feel the breath coming in, move with the breath, let your consciousness go deep with the breath. Then let it move out. Go on moving with your breath. Be alert!

Buddha is reported to have said, "Don't miss even a single breath. If a single breath is missed physiologically, you will be dead, and if a single breath is missed in awareness, you will be missing the center, you will be dead inside." So Buddha said, "Breath is essential for the life of the body, and awareness of the breath is essential for the life of the inner center."

Breathe, be aware. And if you are trying to be aware of your breathing, you cannot think, because the mind cannot do two things simultaneously— thinking and witnessing. The very phenomenon of witnessing is absolutely, diametrically opposite to thinking, so you cannot do both. Just as you cannot be both alive and dead, as you cannot be both asleep and awake, you cannot be both thinking and witnessing. Witness anything, and thinking will stop. Thinking comes in, and witnessing disappears.

> Just as you cannot be both alive and dead, as you cannot be both asleep and awake, you cannot be both thinking and witnessing. Witness anything, and thinking will stop. Thinking comes in, and witnessing disappears.

Witnessing is a passive awareness, with no action inside. Awareness itself is not an action.

One day Mulla Nasruddin was very much worried, in deep brooding. Anyone could look at his face and feel that he was lost somewhere in thoughts, very tense, in anguish. His wife became alarmed. She asked, "What are you doing, Nasruddin? What are you thinking? What is the problem, why are you so worried?"

The Mulla opened his eyes and said, "This is the ultimate problem. I am thinking about how one knows when one is dead. How does one know that one is dead? If I am to die, how will I recognize that I am dead?—because I have not known death. Recognition means you have known something before.

"I see you and recognize that you are A, or B or C, because I have known you. Death I have not known," said the Mulla. "And when it comes, how am I to recognize it? That is the problem, and I am very much worried. And when I am dead, I cannot ask anyone else, so that door is also closed. I cannot refer to some scripture, no teacher can be of any help."

The wife laughed and said, "You are unnecessarily worrying. When death comes, one knows immediately. When death comes to you, you will know because you will become just cold, ice-cold." Mulla was relieved—a certain sign, the key, was in his hand.

After two or three months he was cutting wood in the forest. It was a winter morning and everything was cold. Suddenly he remembered, and he felt his hands—they were cold. He said, "Okay! Now death is coming, and I am so far from my house that I cannot even inform anyone. Now what am I to do? I forgot to ask my wife. She told me how one will feel, but what is one to do when death comes? Now no one is here, and everything is going just cold."

Then he remembered. He had seen many persons dead, so he thought, "It is good to lie down." That is all that he has seen dead persons do, so he lies down. Of course, he becomes more cold, he feels more cold—death is upon him. His donkey is just resting by his side under the tree. Two wolves, thinking that Mulla is dead, attack his donkey. Mulla opens his eyes and sees, and he thinks, "Dead men cannot do anything. Had I been alive, wolves, you couldn't have taken such liberties with my donkey. But now I cannot do anything. Dead men are never reported to have done anything. I can only witness."

If you become dead to your past, totally dead, then you can only witness. What else can you do? Witnessing means becoming dead to your past—memory, thought, everything. Then in the present moment, what can you do? You can only witness. No judgment is possible—judgment is possible only against past experiences. No evaluation is possible—evaluation is possible only against past evaluations. No thinking is possible—thinking is possible only if the past is there, brought into the present. So what can you do? You can witness.

In the old Sanskrit literature, the teacher is defined as the death—*acharya mrityuh*. In the Katha Upanishad, Nachiketa is sent to Yama, the god of death, to be taught. And when Yama, the death god, offers many, many allurements to Nachiketa—"Take this, take the kingdom, take so much wealth, so many horses, so many elephants, this and this," a long list of things—Nachiketa says, "I have come to learn what death is, because unless I know what death is, I cannot know what life is."

So a teacher was known in the old days as a person who can become a death to the disciple—who can help you to die so that you can be reborn. Nicodemus asked Jesus, "How can I attain to the kingdom of God?" Jesus said, "Unless you die first, nothing can be attained. Unless you are reborn, nothing can be attained."

And this being reborn is not an event, it is a continuous process. One has to be reborn every moment. It is not that you are reborn once and then it is okay and finished. Life is a continuous birth, and death is also continuous. You have to die once because you have not lived at all. If you live, then you will have to die every moment. Die every moment to the past whatsoever it has been, a heaven or a hell. Whatsoever—die to it, and be fresh and young and reborn into the moment. Witness now—and you can only witness now if you are fresh.

TENSION AND RELAXATION

Now one thing has to be understood. The hypnotists have discovered a fundamental law; they call it the law of reverse effect. If you try hard to do something without understanding the fundamentals, just the opposite will be the result.

It is like when you are learning how to ride a bicycle. You are on a silent road, no traffic, early in the morning, and you see a red milestone just standing there by the side of the road. A sixty-foot-wide road and just a small milestone, and you become afraid: you may get to the milestone and you may hit it. Now you forget about the sixty-foot-wide road. In fact, even if you go blindfolded, there is not much chance of your encountering the milestone, crashing into it, but with open eyes now the whole road is forgotten; you have become focused. In the first place, that redness is very focusing. And you are so much afraid!—you want to avoid it. You have forgotten that you are on a bicycle, you have forgotten everything. Now the only problem for you is how to avoid this stone; otherwise you may harm yourself, you may crash into it.

Now the crash is absolutely inevitable; you are bound to crash into the stone. And then you will be surprised: "I tried so hard not to hit it." In fact it is *because* you tried hard that you ran into the stone. The closer you come, the harder you try to avoid it; but the harder you try to avoid it, the more focused you become on it. It becomes a hypnotic force, it hypnotizes you. It becomes like a magnet.

It is a fundamental law in life. Many people try avoiding many things and they fall into those same things. Try to avoid anything with great effort and you are bound to fall into the same pit. You cannot avoid it; that is not the way to avoid it.

Be relaxed. Don't try hard, because it is through relaxation that you can become aware, not by trying hard. Be calm, quiet, silent.

WHAT IS YOUR TENSION? Your identification with all kinds of thoughts, fears—death, bankruptcy, the dollar going down, all kinds of fears are there. These are your tensions, and they affect your body also. Your body also becomes tense, because body and mind are not two separate entities. Bodymind is a single system, so when the mind becomes tense, the body becomes tense.

You can start with awareness; then awareness takes you away from the mind and the identifications with the mind. Naturally, the body starts relaxing. You are no longer attached, and tensions cannot exist in the light of awareness.

You can start from the other end also. Just relax, let all tensions drop . . . and as you relax you will be surprised that a certain awareness is arising in you. They are inseparable. But to start from awareness is easier; to start with relaxation is a little difficult, because

> What is your tension? Your identification with all kinds of thoughts, fears—death, bankruptcy, the dollar going down, all kinds of fears are there. These are your tensions, and they affect your body also.

even the effort to relax creates a certain tension.

There is an American book—and if you want to discover all kinds of stupid books, America is the place. The moment I saw the title of the book, I could not believe it. The title is *You Must Relax*. Now if the *must* is there, how can you relax? The *must* will make you tense; the very word immediately creates tension. *Must* comes like a commandment from God. Perhaps the person who is writing the book knows nothing about relaxation and knows nothing about the complexities of relaxation.

In the East we have never started meditation from relaxation; we have started meditation from awareness. Then relaxation comes on its own accord, you don't have to bring it. If you have to bring it, there will be a certain tension. It should come on its own; then only will it be pure relaxation. And it comes. . . .

> As you relax, you will be surprised that a certain awareness is arising in you. They are inseparable. But to start from awareness is easier; to start with relaxation is a little difficult, because even the effort to relax creates a certain tension.

If you want to, you can try from relaxation, but not according to American advisers. In the sense of experience of the inner world, America is the most childish place on the earth. Europe is a little older—but the East has lived for thousands of years in the search for its inner self.

America is only three hundred years old—in the life of a nation three hundred years are nothing—hence, America is the greatest danger to the world. Nuclear weapons in the hands of children . . . Russia will behave more rationally; it is an old and ancient land and has all the experiences of a long history. In America there is no history.

Everybody knows his father's name, forefather's name, and that's all. There your family tree ends.

America is just a baby—or not even a baby, just in the womb. Compared to societies like India and China, it has just been conceived. It is dangerous to give these people nuclear weapons.

There are political, religious, sociological, economical problems, all torturing you. To begin with relaxation is difficult; hence, in the East we have never started from relaxation. But if you want to, I have a certain idea how you should start. I have been working with Western people and I have become aware that they don't belong to the East and they don't know the Eastern current of consciousness; they are coming from a different tradition that has never known any awareness.

For the Western people especially, I have created meditations like Dynamic Meditation.* While I was conducting camps of meditators, I used a gibberish meditation and the Kundalini Meditation. If you want to start from relaxation, then these meditations have to be done first. They will take out all tensions from your mind and body, and then relaxation is easy. You don't know how much you are holding in, and that this is the cause of tension.

When I was allowing gibberish meditation in the camps in the mountains . . . It is difficult to allow it in the cities because the neighbors start going mad. They start phoning the police and saying, "Our whole life is being destroyed!" They don't know that if they would participate in their own houses, their lives would come out of the insanity in which they are living. But they are not even aware of their insanity.

The gibberish meditation was that everybody was allowed to say loudly whatever came into his mind. And it was such a joy to hear what people were saying, irrelevant, absurd—because I was the only witness. People were doing all kinds of things, and the only condition

*See *Meditation: The First and Last Freedom*.

was that you should not touch anybody else. You could do whatever you wanted. . . . Somebody was standing on his head, somebody had thrown off his clothes and become naked, running all around—for the whole hour.

One man used to sit every day in front of me—he must have been a broker or something—and as the meditation would begin, first he would smile, just at the idea of what he was going to do. Then he would take up his phone: "Hello, hello . . ." From the corner of his eyes he would go on looking at me. I would avoid looking at him so as not to disturb his meditation. He was selling his shares, purchasing . . . the whole hour he was on the phone.

Everybody was doing the strange things that they were holding back. When the meditation would end, there were ten minutes for relaxation, and you could see that in those ten minutes people fell down—not with any effort, but because they were utterly tired. All the rubbish had been thrown out, so they had a certain cleanliness, and they relaxed. Thousands of people . . . and you could not even think that there were a thousand people.

People used to come to me and say, "Prolong those ten minutes, because in our whole life we have never seen such relaxation, such joy. We had never thought we would ever understand what awareness is, but we felt it was coming."

So if you want to start with relaxation, first you have to go through a cathartic process—Dynamic Meditation, Kundalini Meditation, or gibberish.

You may not know from where this word *gibberish* comes; it comes from a Sufi mystic whose name was Jabbar—and that was his only meditation. Whoever would come, he would say, "Sit down and start"—and people knew what he meant. He never talked, he never gave any discourses; he simply taught people gibberish.

For example, once in a while he would give people a demonstration. For half an hour he would talk all kinds of nonsense in nobody knows what language. It was not a language; he would go on teaching people just whatever came to his mind. That was his only teaching—and to those who had understood it, he would simply say, "Sit down and start."

But Jabbar helped many people to become utterly silent. How long you can go on?—the mind becomes empty. Slowly, slowly, a deep nothingness . . . and in that nothingness a flame of awareness. It is always present, surrounded by your gibberish. The gibberish has to be taken out; that is your poison.

The same is true about the body—your body has tensions. Just start making any movements that the body wants to make. You should not manipulate it. If it wants to dance, it wants to jog, it wants to run, it wants to roll down on the ground—you should not *do* it, you should simply allow it. Tell the body, "You are free, do whatever you want"—and you will be surprised: "My God! All these things the body wanted to do but I was holding back, and that was the tension."

So there are two kinds of tension, the body tensions and the mind tensions. Both have to be released before you can start relaxation, which will bring you to awareness.

But beginning from awareness is far easier, and particularly for those who can understand the process of awareness, which is simple. The whole day you are using it about things—cars, in the traffic—even in the city traffic you survive! And it is absolutely mad.

Just a few days ago I read about Athens. The government made a spe-

> There are two kinds of tension, the body tensions and the mind tensions. Both have to be released before you can start relaxation, which will bring you to awareness. But beginning from awareness is far easier, and particularly for those who can understand the process.

cial seven-day competition for the taxi drivers, and they had created golden trophies for the three drivers who were the best at following traffic rules. But in the whole of Athens they could not find a single person! The police were getting worried; the days were almost finished, and on the last day they wanted to find anyhow three drivers—they may not be perfect, but those prizes had to be distributed.

One man they found was following the traffic rules exactly, so they were happy. They rushed toward him with the trophy, but seeing the police coming, the man went against a red light! Who wants to get unnecessarily into trouble? The police were shouting, "Wait!"—but he did not listen, he was immediately gone, against the light. They tried with two other people, but nobody would stop, seeing the police. So after seven days' effort, those three prizes are still sitting in the headquarters of the police, and Athens is going on as rejoicingly as ever. . . .

You are using awareness without being aware of it, but only about outside things.

It is the same awareness that has to be used for the inside traffic. When you close your eyes, there is a traffic of thoughts, emotions, dreams, imaginations. All kinds of things start flashing by. What you have been doing in the outside world, do exactly the same with the inside world, and you will become a witness. And once tasted, the joy of being a witness is so great, so otherworldly, that you would like to go more and more in. Whenever you find time, you would like to go more and more in.

It is not a question of any posture; it is not a question of any temple, of

Sitting in a public bus or in a railway train, when you have nothing to do, just close your eyes. It will save your eyes from being tired from looking outside, and it will give you time enough to watch yourself.

any church or synagogue. Sitting in a public bus or in a railway train, when you have nothing to do, just close your eyes. It will save your eyes from being tired from looking outside, and it will give you time enough to watch yourself. Those moments will become moments of the most beautiful experiences.

And slowly, slowly, as awareness grows, your whole personality starts changing. From unawareness to awareness is the greatest quantum leap.

MIND AND MEDITATION

When the mind is without thought, it is meditation.

The mind is without thought in two states—either in deep sleep or in meditation. If you are aware and thoughts disappear, it is meditation. If thoughts disappear and you become unaware, it is deep sleep.

Deep sleep and meditation have something similar and something different. One thing is similar—in both, thinking disappears. One thing is dissimilar—in deep sleep, awareness also disappears, but in meditation it remains. So meditation is equal to deep sleep plus awareness. You are relaxed, as in deep sleep, and yet aware, fully awake—and that brings you to the door of the mysteries.

In deep sleep you move into no-mind, but unawares. You don't know where you are being taken, although in the morning you will feel the impact and the effect. If it has been a really

> Deep sleep and meditation have something similar and something different. One thing is similar— in both, thinking disappears. One thing is dissimilar—in deep sleep, awareness also disappears, but in meditation it remains.

beautiful, deep sleep, with no dreams disturbing you, in the morning you will feel fresh, rejuvenated, alive, again young, again full of zest and juice. But you don't know how it happened, where you had gone. You were taken in a kind of deep coma, as if some anesthetic was given to you and then you were taken to some other plane from where you have come fresh, young, rejuvenated.

In meditation it happens without anesthesia.

So, meditation means remaining as relaxed as you are in deep sleep and yet alert. Keep awareness there—let thoughts disappear, but awareness has to be retained. And this is not difficult, it is just that we have not tried it, that's all. It is like swimming: if you have not tried it, it looks difficult. It looks dangerous too, and you cannot believe how people can swim because you simply drown! But once you have tried a little bit, it comes easily; it is very natural.

Now one scientist in Japan has proved it experimentally that a child of six months of age is capable of swimming; just the opportunity has to be given. He has taught many children of six months of age to swim; he has done a miracle! He says he will be trying with smaller children too. It is as if the art of swimming is in-built; we just have to give it an opportunity and it starts functioning. That's why, once you have learned swimming, you never forget it. You may not swim for forty years, fifty years, but you cannot forget it. It is not something accidental, it is something natural; that's why you cannot forget it.

> Meditation means remaining as relaxed as you are in deep sleep and yet alert. Keep awareness there—let thoughts disappear, but awareness has to be retained. And this is not difficult, it is just that we have not tried it, that's all.

Meditation is similar; it is something in-built. You just have to create a space for it to function; just give it a chance.

WHAT IS MIND? MIND IS NOT A THING, BUT AN EVENT. A thing has substance in it, an event is just a process. A thing is like a rock, an event is like a wave—it exists, but is not substantial. It is just the event between the wind and the ocean, a process, a phenomenon.

This is the first thing to be understood, that mind is a process like a wave or like a river, but it has no substance in it. If it has substance, then it cannot be dissolved. If it has no substance, it can disappear without leaving a single trace behind.

> *Meditation is something in-built. You just have to create a space for it to function, just give it a chance.*

When a wave disappears into the ocean, what is left behind? Nothing, not even a trace. So those who have known, they say mind is like a bird flying into the sky—no footprints are left behind, not even a trace. The bird flies but leaves no path, no footprints.

The mind is just a process. In fact, mind doesn't exist—only thoughts, thoughts moving so fast that you think and feel that something exists there in continuity. One thought comes, another thought comes, another, and they go on . . . the gap is so small you cannot see the interval between one thought and another. So two thoughts become joined, they become a continuity, and because of that continuity you think there is a mind.

There are thoughts—no "mind." Just as there are electrons—no "matter." Thought is the electron of the mind. Just like a crowd . . . a crowd exists in a sense, doesn't exist in another. Only individuals exist, but many individuals together give the feeling as if they are one. A nation exists and exists not—only individuals are there. Individuals are the electrons of a nation, of a community, of a crowd.

Thoughts exist—mind doesn't exist; mind is just the appearance. And when you look into the mind deeper, it disappears. Then there are thoughts, but when the "mind" has disappeared and only individual thoughts exist, many things are immediately solved. The first thing is that immediately you come to know that thoughts are like clouds—they come and go, and you are the sky. When there is no mind, immediately the perception comes that you are no longer involved in the thoughts—thoughts are there, pass-

> The mind is just a process. In fact, mind doesn't exist—only thoughts, thoughts moving so fast that you think and feel that something exists there in continuity.

ing through you like clouds passing through the sky, or the wind passing through the trees. Thoughts are passing through you, and they can pass because you are a vast emptiness. There is no hindrance, no obstacle. No wall exists to prevent them; you are not a walled phenomenon. Your sky is the infinitely open; thoughts come and go.

And once you start feeling that thoughts come and go, and you are the watcher, the witness, the mastery of the mind is achieved.

Mind cannot be controlled in the ordinary sense. In the first place, because it is not, how can you control it? In the second place, who will control the mind? Because nobody exists beyond the mind—and when I say nobody exists, I mean that *nobody* exists beyond the mind, a nothingness. Who will control the mind? If somebody is controlling the

> There are thoughts—no "mind." Just as there are electrons—no "matter." Thought is the electron of the mind.

mind, then it will be only a part, a fragment of the mind controlling another fragment of the mind. That is what the ego is.

Mind cannot be controlled in that way. It is not, and there is nobody to control it. The inner emptiness can see but cannot control. It can look but cannot control—but the very look *is the control,* the very phenomenon of observation, of witnessing, becomes the mastery because the mind disappears.

It is just as if in a dark night you are running fast because you have become afraid of somebody following you. And that somebody is nothing but your own shadow, and the more you run, the closer to you is the shadow. How fast you run makes no difference; the shadow is there. Whenever you look back, the shadow is there. That is not the way to escape from it, and that is not the way to control it. You will have to look deeper into the shadow. Stand still and look deeper into the shadow and the shadow disappears because the shadow is not; it is just an absence of light.

Mind is nothing but the absence of your presence. When you sit silently, when you look deep into the mind, the mind simply disappears. Thoughts will remain, they are existential, but mind will not be found.

But when the mind is gone, then a second perception becomes possible: you can see that thoughts are not yours. Of course they come, and sometimes they rest a little while in you, and then they go. You may be a resting place, but they don't originate in you. Have you ever noticed that not even a single thought has arisen out of you? Not a

> When you look into the mind deeper, it disappears. Then there are thoughts, but when the "mind" has disappeared and only individual thoughts exist, you come to know that thoughts are like clouds—they come and go, and you are the sky.

single thought has come through your being; they always come from the outside. They don't belong to you—rootless, homeless, they hover. Sometimes they rest in you, that's all, like a cloud resting on top of a hill. Then they will move on their own; you need not do anything. If you simply watch, control is attained.

The word *control* is not very good, because words cannot be very good. Words belong to the mind, to the world of thoughts. Words cannot be very, very penetrating; they are shallow. The word *control* is not good because there is nobody to control and there is nobody to be controlled. But tentatively, it helps to understand a certain thing that happens: when you look

> Mind is nothing but the absence of your presence. When you sit silently, when you look deep into the mind, the mind simply disappears. Thoughts will remain, they are existential, but mind will not be found.

deeply, mind is controlled—suddenly you have become the master. Thoughts are there, but they are no longer masters of you. They cannot do anything to you, they simply come and go; you remain untouched just like a lotus flower amidst rainfall. Drops of water fall on the petals but they go on slipping, they don't even touch. The lotus remains untouched.

That's why in the East the lotus became so significant, became so symbolic. The greatest symbol that has come out of the East is the lotus. It carries the whole meaning of the Eastern consciousness. It says, "Be like a lotus, that's all. Remain untouched and you are in control. Remain untouched and you are the master."

So from one standpoint, the mind is like waves—a disturbance. When the ocean is calm and quiet, undisturbed, the waves are not there. When the ocean is disturbed in a tide or strong wind, when tremendous waves arise and the whole surface is just a chaos, the mind

> Have you ever noticed that not even a single thought has arisen out of you? Not a single thought has come through your being, they always come from the outside. They don't belong to you— rootless, homeless, they hover. Sometimes they rest in you, that's all.

from one standpoint exists. These are all metaphors just to help you to understand a certain quality inside, which cannot be said through words. These metaphors are poetic. If you try to understand them with sympathy, you will attain an understanding, but if you try to understand them logically, you will miss the point. They are metaphors.

Mind is a disturbance of consciousness, just as waves are a disturbance of the ocean. Something foreign has entered—the wind. Something from the outside has happened to the ocean, or to the consciousness—the wind, or the thoughts, and there is chaos. But the chaos is always on the surface. The waves are always on the surface. There are no waves in the depths—cannot be, because in the depths the wind cannot enter. So everything is just on the surface. If you move inward, control is attained. If you move inward from the surface you go to the center—suddenly, the surface may still be disturbed but *you* are not disturbed.

The whole of the science of meditation is nothing but centering, moving toward the center, getting rooted there, abiding there. And from there the whole perspective changes. Now the waves may still be there, but they don't reach you. And now you can see they don't belong to you, it is just a conflict on the surface with something foreign.

And from the center, when you look, by and by the conflict ceases. By and by you relax. By and by you accept that of course there is a strong wind and waves will arise, but you are not worried, and when you are not worried, even waves can be enjoyed. Nothing is wrong in them.

The problem arises when you are also on the surface. You are in a small boat on the surface, and a strong wind comes and it is high tide and the whole ocean goes mad—of course, you are worried, you are scared to death! You are in danger; any moment the waves can overturn your small boat; any moment death can occur. What can you do with your small boat? How can you control anything? If you start fighting with the waves, you will be defeated.

> The whole of the science of meditation is nothing but centering, moving toward the center, getting rooted there, abiding there. And from there the whole perspective changes.

Fight won't help; you will have to accept the waves. In fact, if you can accept the waves and let your boat, however small, move with them and not against them, then there is no danger. Waves are there; you simply allow. You simply allow yourself to move with them, not against them. You become part of them. Then tremendous happiness arises.

That is the whole art of surfing—moving with the waves, not against them. With them—so much so, that you are not different from them. Surfing can become a great meditation. It can give you glimpses of the inner because it is not a fight, it is a let-go. Once you know that, even waves can be enjoyed . . . and that can be known when you look at the whole phenomenon from the center.

Just as if you are a traveler in the forest and clouds have gathered, and there is much lightning, and you have lost the path and you are trying to hurry toward home. This is what is happening on the surface—a traveler lost, many clouds, much lightning; soon there will be a tremendous rain. You are seeking home, the safety of home—

then suddenly you reach there. Now you sit inside, now you wait
for the rains—now you can enjoy. Now the lightning has a beauty
of its own. It was not so when you were outside, lost in the forest,
but now, sitting inside the house, the whole phenomenon is tremendously beautiful. Now the rain comes and you enjoy. Now the lightning is there and you enjoy, and great thunder in the clouds, and you
enjoy because now you are safe inside.

Once you reach the center, you start enjoying whatsoever happens on the surface. So the whole thing is not to fight on the surface,
but rather slip into the center. Then there is mastery, and not a control that has been forced, a mastery that happens spontaneously when
you are centered.

Centering in consciousness is the mastery of the mind.

So don't try to "control the mind"—the language can mislead
you. Nobody can control, and those who try to control will go mad;
they will simply go neurotic, because trying to control the mind is
nothing but a part of the mind trying to control another part of the
mind.

Who are you, who is trying to control? You are also a wave—a
religious wave of course, trying to control the mind. And there are
irreligious waves—there is sex and there is anger and there is jealousy
and possessiveness and hatred, and millions of irreligious waves. And
then there are religious waves—meditation, love, compassion. But
these are all on the surface, of the surface, and on the surface. Religious or irreligious makes no difference.

Real religion is at the center, and in the perspective that happens
through the center. Sitting inside your home, you look at your own
surface—everything changes because your perspective is new. Suddenly you are the master. In fact, you are so much in control that
you can leave the surface uncontrolled. This is subtle—you are so in
control, so rooted, not worried about the surface, that in fact you
can enjoy the waves and the tides and the storm. It is beautiful, it
gives energy, it gives a strength—there is nothing to be worried about
it. Only weaklings worry about thoughts. Only weaklings worry

about the mind. <u>Stronger people simply absorb the whole, and they</u> <u>are richer for it. Stronger people simply never reject anything.</u>

Rejection is out of weakness—you are afraid. Stronger people would like to absorb everything that life gives. <u>Religious, irreligious,</u> <u>moral, immoral, divine, devilish—it makes no difference; the stronger</u> <u>person absorbs everything.</u> And he is richer for it. He has a totally different depth that ordinary religious people cannot have; they are poor and shallow.

Watch <u>ordinary religious people</u> going to the temple and to the mosque and to the church. You will always find <u>very, very shallow</u> <u>people with no depth.</u> Because they have rejected parts of themselves, they have become crippled. They are in a certain way paralyzed.

Nothing is wrong in the mind, nothing is wrong in the thoughts. If anything is wrong, it is remaining on the surface—because then you don't know the whole and unnecessarily suffer because of the part and the partial perception. A whole perception is needed, and that is possible only from the center—because from the center you can look all around in all dimensions, all directions, at the whole periphery of your being. And it is vast. In fact, it is the same as the periphery of existence. Once you are centered, by and by you become wider and wider and bigger and bigger, and you end with being the whole, not less than that.

From another standpoint, mind is like dust a traveler gathers on his clothes. And you have been traveling and traveling and traveling for millions of lives, and never taken a bath. Much dust has collected, naturally—nothing wrong in it; it has to be so—layers of dust and you think those layers are your personality. You have become so iden-

> Mind is like dust a traveler gathers on his clothes. And you have been traveling and traveling and traveling for millions of lives, and never taken a bath.

tified with them, you have lived with those layers of dust so long, that they look like your skin. You have become identified.

Mind is the past, the memory, the dust. Everybody has to gather it—if you travel, you will gather dust. But no need to be identified with it, no need to become one with it, because if you become one with it, then you will be in trouble because you are not the dust, you are consciousness. Says Omar Khayyám, "Dust unto dust." When a man dies, what happens?—dust returns unto dust. If you are just dust, then everything will return to the dust; nothing will be left behind. But are you just dust, layers of dust, or is something inside you that is not dust at all, not of the earth at all?

That's your consciousness, your awareness. Awareness is your being, consciousness is your being, and the dust that awareness collects around it is your mind.

There are two ways to deal with this dust. The ordinary "religious" way is to clean the clothes, rub your body hard. But those methods cannot help much. Howsoever you clean your clothes, the clothes have become so dirty they are beyond redemption. You cannot clean them; on the contrary, whatsoever you do may make them more unclean.

It happened:

Mulla Nasruddin came once to me, and he is a drunkard. His hands shake—eating, drinking tea, everything falls on his clothes, so all his clothes were stained with tea and food and this and that. So I told Nasruddin, "Why don't you go to the chemist and find something? There are solutions and these stains can be washed."

He went. After seven days he came back; his clothes were in a worse condition, worse than before. I asked, "What happened? Didn't you go to the chemist?" He said, "I went. And that chemical solution is wonderful—it works. All the stains of tea and food are gone. Now I need another solution, because that solution has left its own stains."

Religious people supply you with soaps and chemical solutions, instructions on how to wash away the dirt, but then those solutions leave their own stains. That's why an immoral person can become moral but remains dirty—now in moral way, but he remains dirty. Sometimes the situation is even worse than before.

An immoral man is in many ways innocent, less egoistic. A moral man has all the immorality inside the mind, and he has gathered new things—those are the moralistic, the puritan, the egoistic attitudes. He feels superior; he feels he is the chosen one. And everybody else is condemned to hell; only he is going to heaven. And all the immorality remains inside, because you cannot control the mind from the surface; there is no way. It simply doesn't happen that way. Only one control exists, and that is the perception from the center.

Mind is like dust gathered through millions of journeys. The real religious standpoint, the radical religious standpoint against the ordinary, is to simply throw away the clothes. Don't bother to wash them, they cannot be washed. Simply move like a snake out of his old skin and don't even look back.

From still another standpoint, mind is the past, the memory, all the experiences accumulated, in a sense. All that you have done, all that you have thought, all that you have desired, all that you have dreamed—everything, your total past, your memory—memory is mind. And unless you get rid of memory, you will not be able to master the mind.

How to get rid of memory? It is always there, following you. In fact, you *are* the memory, so how to get rid of it? Who are you except your memories? When I ask, "Who are you?" you tell me your name—that is your memory. Your parents gave you that name some time back. I ask you, "Who are you?" and you tell about your family, your father, your mother—that is a memory. I ask you, "Who are you?" and you tell me about your education, your degrees, that you have a master of arts, or you are a Ph.D., or you are an engineer or an architect. That is a memory.

When I ask you, "Who are you?" if really you look inside, your only answer can be "I don't know." Whatsoever you will say will be the memory, not you. The only real, authentic answer can be "I don't know," because to know oneself is the last thing. I can answer who I am, but I will not answer. You cannot answer who you are, but you are ready with the answer. Those who know, they keep silent about this. Because if all the memory is discarded, and all the language is discarded, then who I am cannot be said. I can look into you, I can give you a gesture; I can be with you, with my total being— that is my answer. But the answer cannot be given in words because whatsoever is given in words will be part of memory, part of mind, not of consciousness.

> You were born in a certain family, but this is not you, it has happened to you, an event outside of you. Of course somebody has given a name to you, it has its utility, but the name is not you. Of course you have a form, but the form is not you, the form is just the house you happen to be in.

How to get rid of the memories? Watch them, witness them. And always remember, "This has happened to me, but this is not me." Of course you were born in a certain family, but this is not you; it has happened to you, an event outside of you. Of course somebody has given a name to you; it has its utility, but the name is not you. Of course you have a form, but the form is not you; the form is just the house you happen to be in. The form is just the body that you happen to be in. And the body is given to you by your parents— it is a gift, but is not you.

Watch and discriminate. This is what in the East they call *vivek*, discrimination—you discriminate continuously. Keep on discriminating—a moment comes when you have eliminated all that you are not. Suddenly, in that state, you for the first time face yourself, you encounter your own being. Go on cutting all identities that you are not—the family, the body, the mind. In that emptiness, when everything that was not you has been thrown out, suddenly your being surfaces. For the first time you encounter yourself, and that encounter becomes the mastery.

THINKING CANNOT BE STOPPED—NOT THAT IT DOES NOT STOP, BUT IT CANNOT BE STOPPED. It stops of its own accord. This distinction has to be understood; otherwise you can go mad chasing your mind.

No-mind does not arise by stopping thinking. When the thinking is no more, no-mind is. The very effort to stop will create more anxiety, it will create conflict, it will make you split. You will be in a constant turmoil within. This is not going to help.

And even if you succeed in stopping it forcibly for a few moments, it is not an achievement at all—because those few moments will be almost dead, they will not be alive. You may feel a sort of stillness . . . but not silence. Because a forced stillness is not silence. Underneath it, deep in the unconscious, the repressed mind goes on working.

So, there is no way to stop the mind. But the mind stops—that is certain. It stops of its own accord.

So what to do?—the question is relevant. Watch. Don't try to stop. There is no need to do any action against the mind. In the first place, who will do it? It will be mind fighting mind

> Go on cutting all identities that you are not—the family, the body, the mind. In that emptiness, when everything that was not you has been thrown out, suddenly your being surfaces. For the first time you encounter yourself, and that encounter becomes the mastery.

> *Thinking cannot be stopped—not that it does not stop, but it cannot be stopped. It stops of its own accord. This distinction has to be understood, otherwise you can go mad chasing your mind.*

itself; you will divide your mind into two: one that is trying to be the boss, the top dog, trying to kill the other part of itself—which is absurd. It is a foolish game, it can drive you crazy. Don't try to stop the mind or the thinking—just watch it, allow it. Allow it total freedom. Let it run as fast as it wants; you don't try in any way to control it. You just be a witness.

It is beautiful! Mind is one of the most beautiful mechanisms. Science has not yet been able to create anything parallel to mind. Mind still remains the masterpiece, so complicated, so tremendously powerful, with so many potentialities. Watch it! Enjoy it!

And don't watch like an enemy, because if you look at the mind like an enemy, you cannot watch. You are already prejudiced, you are already *against*. You have already decided that something is wrong with the mind—you have already concluded. And whenever you look at somebody as an enemy, you never look deep, you never look into the eye; you avoid.

Watching the mind means to look at it with deep love, with deep respect, reverence—it is God's gift to you. Nothing is wrong in mind itself. Nothing is wrong in thinking itself. It is a beautiful process, as other processes are. Clouds moving in the sky are beautiful—why not thoughts moving in the inner sky? Flowers coming to the trees are beautiful—why not thoughts flowering in your being? The river running to the ocean is beautiful—why not this stream of thoughts running somewhere to an unknown destiny? Is it not beautiful? Look with deep reverence. Don't be a fighter, be a lover.

Watch the subtle nuances of the mind, the sudden turns, the

beautiful turns. The sudden jumps and leaps, the games that mind goes on playing; the dreams that it weaves—the imagination, the memory, the thousand and one projections that it creates—watch! Standing there aloof, distant, not involved, by and by you will start feeling . . . The deeper your watchfulness becomes, the deeper your awareness becomes, gaps start arising, intervals. One thought goes and another has not come, and there is a gap. One cloud has passed, another is coming, and there is a gap.

In those gaps, for the first time you will have glimpses of no-mind. You will have the taste of no-mind—call it the taste of Zen, or Tao, or Yoga. In those small intervals, suddenly the sky is clear and the sun is shining. Suddenly the world is full of mystery, because all barriers are dropped; the screen on your eyes is no longer there. You see clearly, you see penetratingly. The whole existence becomes transparent.

In the beginning, these will be just rare moments, few and far in between. But they will give you glimpses of what *samadhi* is. Small pools of silence—they will come and they will disappear, but now you know that you are on the right track. You start watching again. When a thought passes, you watch it; when an interval passes, you watch it. Clouds are also beautiful; sunshine also is beautiful. Now you are not a chooser. Now you don't have a fixed mind. You don't say, "I would like only the intervals." That is stupid, because once you become attached to wanting only the intervals, you have decided again *against* thinking. And then those

> Mind is one of the most beautiful mechanisms. Science has not yet been able to create anything parallel to it. Mind remains the masterpiece—so complicated, so tremendously powerful, with so many potentialities. Watch it! Enjoy it!

intervals will disappear. They happen only when you are distant, aloof. They happen, they cannot be brought. They happen, you cannot force them to happen. They are spontaneous happenings.

> ➴
>
> When a thought passes, you watch it, when an interval passes, you watch it. Clouds are also beautiful, sunshine also is beautiful. Now you are not a chooser. Now you don't have a fixed mind.

Go on watching. Let thoughts come and go—wherever they want to go. Nothing is wrong! Don't try to manipulate and don't try to direct. Let thoughts move in total freedom. And then bigger intervals will be coming. You will be blessed with small *satoris*. Sometimes minutes will pass and no thought will be there; there will be no traffic—a total silence, undisturbed.

When the bigger gaps come, you will have a new clarity arising. You will not only have clarity to see into the world, you will be able to see into the inner world. With the first gaps you will see into the world—trees will be more green than they look right now, you will be surrounded by an infinite music, the music of the spheres. You will suddenly be in the presence of godliness—ineffable, mysterious. Touching you, although you cannot grasp it. Within your reach and yet beyond. With the bigger gaps, the same will happen inside. God will not only be outside, you will suddenly be surprised—he is inside also. He is not only in the seen, he is in the seer also—within and without. By and by . . .

But don't get attached to that, either. Attachment is the food for the mind to continue. Nonattached witnessing is the way to stop it without any effort to stop it. And when you start enjoying those blissful moments, your capacity to retain them for longer periods arises. Finally, eventually, one day you become master. Then, when you want to think, you think; if thought is needed, you use it. If thought is not needed, you allow it to rest. Not that mind is simply no longer there—mind is there, but you can use it or not use it. Now it is your decision, just like legs: if you want to run you use them; if you don't want to run, you simply rest. The legs are there. In the same way, mind is always there.

When I am talking to you, I am using the mind—there is no other way to talk. When I am answering your questions, I am using the mind—there is no other way. I have to respond and relate, and mind is a beautiful mechanism. When I am not talking to you and I am alone, there is no mind—because it is a medium to relate through. When I sit alone, it is not needed.

You have not given it a rest; hence, the mind becomes mediocre. Continuously used, tired, it goes on and on and on. Day it works, night it works—in the day you think, in the night you dream. Day in, day out, it goes on working. If you live for seventy or eighty years, it will be continuously working.

Look at the delicacy and the endurability of the mind—so delicate! In a small head all the libraries of the world can be contained; all that has ever been written can be contained in one single mind. Tremendous is the capacity of the mind—and in such a small space! and not making much noise. If scientists someday become capable of creating a computer parallel to mind . . . computers are there, but they are not yet minds. They are still mechanisms, they have no organic unity; they don't have any center yet. If someday it becomes possible—and it is possible that scientists may someday be able to create minds—then you will know how much space that computer will take, and how much noise it will make!

Mind is making almost no noise; it goes on working silently. And such a servant!—for seventy, eighty years. And then too, when you are dying, your body may be old but your mind remains young. Its capacity remains yet the same. Sometimes, if you have used it rightly, it even increases with your age—because the more you know, the more you understand. The more you have experienced and lived, the more capable your mind becomes. When you die, everything in your body is ready to die—except the mind.

That's why in the East we say the mind leaves the body and enters another womb, because it is not yet ready to die. The rebirth is of the mind. And once you have attained the state of no-mind, then there will be no rebirth. Then you will simply die. And with your dying, everything will be dissolved—your body, your mind— only your witnessing soul will remain. That is beyond time and space. Then you become one with existence; then you are no longer separate from it. The separation comes from the mind.

But there is no way to stop it forcibly—don't be violent. Move lovingly, with a deep reverence, and it will start happening of its own accord. You just watch, and don't be in a hurry.

The modern mind is in much hurry. It wants instant methods for stopping the mind. Hence, drugs have appeal. You can force the mind to stop by using chemicals, drugs, but again you are being violent with the mechanism. It is not good, it is destructive. In this way you are not going to become a master. You may be able to stop the mind through drugs, but then drugs will become your master—you are not going to become the master. You have simply changed your bosses, and you have changed for the worse. Now the drugs will hold the power over you, they will possess you; without them you will be nowhere.

Meditation is not an effort against

> The modern mind is in much hurry. It wants instant methods for stopping the mind. Hence, drugs have appeal. You can force the mind to stop by using chemicals, drugs, but you are being violent with the mechanism. It is destructive. In this way you are not going to become a master.

the mind, it is a way of understanding the mind. It is a loving way of witnessing the mind—but of course, one has to be patient. This mind that you are carrying in your head has arisen over centuries, millennia. Your small mind carries the whole experience of humanity. And not only of humanity—of animals, of birds, of plants, of rocks; you have passed through all those experiences. All that has happened up to now has happened in you also.

In a small nutshell, you carry the whole experience of existence. That's what your mind is. In fact, to say it is yours is not right. It is collective; it belongs to us all. Modern psychology has been approaching it, particularly Jungian analysis has been approaching it, and they have started feeling something like a collective unconscious. Your mind is not yours—it belongs to us all. Our bodies are very separate; our minds are not so separate. Our bodies are clearly separate, our minds overlap—and our souls are one.

Bodies are separate, minds overlapping, and souls are one. I don't have a different soul and you don't have a different soul. At the very center of existence we meet and are one. That's what "God" is—the meeting point of all. Between the God and the world—the "world" means the bodies—is mind.

Mind is a bridge, a bridge between the body and the soul, between the world and God. Don't try to destroy it!

Many have tried to destroy it through Yoga. That is a misuse of Yoga. Many have tried to destroy it through body postures, breathing—that too brings subtle chemical changes inside. For example, if you stand on your head in *shirshasan,* in the headstand, you can destroy the mind very easily. Because when the blood rushes too much, like a flood, into the head . . . when you stand on your head, that's what you are trying to do. The brain mechanism is delicate. You are flooding it with blood, the delicate tissues will die. That's why you never come across an intelligent yogi. No—yogis are, more or less, stupid. Their bodies are healthy, that's true, strong—but their minds are just dead. You will not see the glimmer of intelligence. You will see a very robust body, animal-like, but somehow the human has disappeared.

Standing on your head, you are forcing your blood into the head through gravitation. The head needs blood, but in a small quantity; and slowly, not floodlike. Against gravitation, little blood reaches to the head, and that too in a silent way. If too much blood is reaching into the head, it is destructive.

Yoga has been used to kill the mind. Breathing can be used to kill the mind—there are rhythms of breath, subtle vibrations of breath, that can be drastic to the delicate mind. The mind can be destroyed through them. These are old tricks. Now the latest tricks are supplied by science: LSD, marijuana, and others; more and more sophisticated drugs will be available sooner or later.

I am not in favor of stopping the mind. I am in favor of watching it. It stops of its own accord—and then it is beautiful. When something happens without any violence, it has a beauty of its own; it has a natural growth. You can force a flower and open it by force, you can pull the petals of a bud and open it by force, but you have destroyed the beauty of the flower. Now it is almost dead. It cannot withstand your violence. The petals will be hanging loose, limp, dying. When the bud opens by its own energy, when it opens of its own accord, then those petals are alive.

The mind is your flowering—don't force it in any way. I am against all force and against all violence, and particularly violence that is directed toward yourself.

Just watch—in deep prayer, love, reverence—and see what happens. Miracles happen of their own accord. There is no need to pull and push.

How to stop thinking? I say just watch, be alert. And drop this idea of stopping, otherwise it will stop the natural transformation of the mind. Drop this idea of stopping! Who are you to stop?

At the most, enjoy. And nothing is wrong—even if immoral thoughts, so-called immoral thoughts, pass through your mind, let them pass. Nothing is wrong. You remain detached, no harm is being done. It is just fiction, you are seeing an inner movie. Allow it its own way and it will lead you, by and by, to the state of no-mind. Watching ultimately culminates in no-mind.

> Even if immoral thoughts, so-called immoral thoughts, pass through your mind, let them pass. Nothing is wrong. You remain detached, no harm is being done. It is just fiction, you are seeing an inner movie.

No-mind is not *against* mind; no-mind is *beyond* mind. No-mind does not come by killing and destroying the mind; no-mind comes when you have understood the mind so totally that thinking is no longer needed—your understanding has replaced it.

THE RUT AND THE WHEEL

Man appears to be in the present, but that is only an appearance. Man lives in the past. Through the present he passes, but he remains rooted in the past. The present is not really time for the ordinary consciousness—for the ordinary consciousness, the past is real time, the present just a passage from the past to the future, just a momentary passage. The past is real and the future also, but the present is unreal for the ordinary consciousness.

Future is nothing but the past extended. Future is nothing but the past projected again and again. The present seems to be nonexistential. If you think of the present, you will not find it at all—because the moment you find it, it has already passed. Just a moment before, when you had not found it, it was in the future.

For a buddha-consciousness, for an awakened being, only the present is existential. For ordinary consciousness, unaware, sleepy like a somnambulist, the past and future are real and the present is unreal. Only when one wakes up is the present real, and the past and future both become unreal.

Why is this so? Why do you live in the past?—because mind is nothing but an accumulation of the past. Mind is memory—all that you have done, all that you have dreamed, all that you wanted to do and could not do, all that you have imagined in the past, is your mind. Mind is a dead entity. If you look through the mind, you will never find the present because the present is life, and life can never be approached through a dead medium. Mind is dead.

Mind is just like dust gathering on a mirror. The more dust gathers, the less the mirror is mirrorlike. And if the layer of dust is thick, as it is on you, then the mirror does not reflect at all.

Everybody gathers dust—not only do you gather, you cling to it; you think it is a treasure. The past is gone—why do you cling to it? You cannot do anything about it, you cannot go back, you cannot undo it—why do you cling to it? It is not a treasure. And if you cling to the past and you think it is a treasure, of course your mind will want to live it again and again in the future. Your future cannot be anything but your modified past—a little refined, a little more decorated, but it is going to be the same because the mind cannot think of the unknown. The mind can only project the known, that which you know.

You fall in love with a woman and the woman dies. Now how are you going to find another woman? The other woman is going to be a modified form of your dead wife; that is the only way you know. Whatsoever you do in the future will be nothing but a continuation of the past. You can change a little—a patch here, a patch there, but the main part will remain just the same.

Somebody asked Mulla Nasruddin when he was lying on his deathbed, "If you are again given a life, how are you going to live it, Nasruddin? Would you make any changes?" Nasruddin pondered with closed eyes, thought, meditated, then opened his eyes and said, "Yes, if I am again given a life, I will part my hair in the middle. That has always been my wish, but my father always insisted that I not do it. And when my father died, the hair had become so conditioned that it could not be parted in the middle."

Don't laugh! If you are asked what you will do again with your life, you will make slight changes just like this. A husband with a slightly different nose, a wife with a little different complexion, a bigger or smaller house—but they are nothing more than parting your hair in the middle, trivia, not essential. Your essential life will remain the same. You have done it many, many times; your essential life has remained the same. Many times you have been given a life. You have lived many times; you are very, very ancient. You are not new on this earth, you are older than the earth because you have lived on other earths also, other planets. You are as old as existence—this is how it should be because you are part of it. You are ancient, but repeating the same pattern again and again. That's

> If you cling to the past and you think it is a treasure, of course your mind will want to live it again and again in the future. Your future cannot be anything but your modified past—a little refined, a little more decorated.

> ≈
>
> You have lived many times; you are very, very ancient. You are ancient, but repeating the same pattern again and again. That's why Hindus call it the wheel of life and death—*wheel* because it goes on repeating itself.

why Hindus call it the wheel of life and death—*wheel* because it goes on repeating itself. It is a repetition: the same spokes come up and go down, go down and come up.

Mind projects itself and mind is the past, so your future is not going to be anything other than the past. And what is the past? What have you done in the past? Whatsoever you have done—good, bad, this, that—whatever you do creates its own repetition. That is the theory of karma. If you were angry the day before yesterday, you created a certain potentiality to be angry again yesterday. Then you repeated it, you gave more energy to the anger. The mood of anger—you rooted it more, you watered it; now today you will repeat it again with more force, with more energy. And then tomorrow you will again be a victim of today.

Each action that you do, or even think about, has its own ways of persisting again and again, because it creates a channel in your being. It starts absorbing energy from you. You are angry, then the mood goes and you think that you are angry no more—then you miss the point. When the mood has gone, nothing has happened; only the wheel has moved and the spoke that was up has gone down. The anger was there on the surface a few minutes ago; the anger has now gone down into the unconscious, into the depth of your being. It will wait for its time to come again. If you have acted according to it, you have reinforced it. Then you have again given a lease for its life. You have given it again a power, an energy. It is throbbing like a seed under the soil, waiting for the right opportunity and season, then it will sprout.

Every action is self-perpetuating, every thought is self-perpetuating. Once you cooperate with it, you are giving energy to it. Sooner or later it will become habitual. You will do it and you will not be the doer; you will do it just because of the force of habit. People say that habit is second nature—this is not exaggeration. On the contrary, this is an understatement! In fact, habit finally becomes first nature and nature becomes secondary. Nature becomes just like an appendix or footnotes in a book, and habit becomes the main body of the book.

You live through the habit—that means that the habit lives basically through you. The habit itself persists, it has an energy of its own. Of course it takes the energy from you, but you cooperated in the past and you are cooperating in the present. By and by, the habit will become the master and you will be just a servant, a shadow. The habit will give the commandment, the order, and you will be just an obedient servant. You will have to follow it.

> Every action is self-perpetuating, every thought is self-perpetuating. Once you cooperate with it, you are giving energy to it. Sooner or later it will become habitual. You will do it and you will not be the doer; you will do it just because of the force of habit.

It happened that one Hindu mystic, Eknath, was going for a pilgrimage. The pilgrimage was going to last for at least one year because he had to visit all the sacred places of the country. Of course, it was a privilege to be with Eknath, so a thousand people were traveling with him. The thief of the town also came and said, "I know that I am a thief and not worthy enough to be a member of your religious group, but give me a chance also. I would like to come for the pilgrimage."

Eknath said, "It will be difficult, because one year is a long time and you may start stealing people's things. You may cause trouble. Please drop this idea." But the thief was insistent. He said, "For one year I will drop stealing, but I have to come. And I promise you that for one year I will not steal a single thing from anybody." Eknath agreed.

But within a week trouble started, and the trouble was this: things started disappearing from people's luggage. And even more puzzling was that nobody was stealing them—things would disappear from somebody's bag and they would be found in somebody else's bag after a few days. The man in whose bag they would be found would say, "I have not done anything. I really don't know how these things have come to be in my bag."

Eknath suspected, so one night he pretended to sleep, but he was awake and he watched. The thief appeared near about midnight, in the middle of the night, and he started changing things from one person's luggage to another person's. Eknath caught him red-handed and said, "What are you doing? And you had promised!"

The thief said, "I am following my promise. I have not stolen a single thing. But this is my old habit . . . in the middle of the night if I don't do some mischief, it is impossible for me to sleep. And for one year, not to sleep? You are a man of compassion. You should be compassionate towards me. And I am not stealing! Things are found again and again; they don't go anywhere but are just exchanged from one person to another. And moreover, after one year I have to start my stealing again, so it will be good practice also."

Habits force you to do certain things; you are a victim. Hindus call it the theory of karma. Each action that you repeat, or each thought—because thought is also a subtle action in the mind—becomes more and more powerful. Then you are in the grip of it. Then you are imprisoned in the habit. Then you live the life of an imprisoned man, a slave. And the imprisonment is subtle; the prison is made of your habits and conditioning and the actions that you have done. It is all around your body and you are entangled in it, but you go on thinking and fooling yourself that you are doing it.

When you get angry, you think you are doing it. You rationalize it and you say that the situation demanded it: "I had to be angry, otherwise the child would go astray. If I were not angry, then things would go wrong, then the office would be in a chaos. The servants won't listen; I had to be angry to manage things. To put the wife in her right place I had to be angry." These are rationalizations—that's how your ego goes on thinking that you are still the boss. But you are not.

Anger comes out of old patterns, out of the past. And when anger comes, you try to find an excuse for it. Psychologists have been experimenting and have come to the same conclusions as the Eastern esoteric psychology: man is a victim, not a master. Psychologists have put people in total isolation, with every comfort possible. Whatsoever was needed was given to them, but they didn't come in any contact with other human beings. They lived in isolation in an airconditioned cell—no work, no trouble, no problem, but the same habits continued. One morning, with no reason now—because every comfort was fulfilled, there was no worry, there was no excuse to be angry—the man would suddenly find that anger was arising.

It is within you. Sometimes, suddenly sadness comes for no apparent reason at all. And sometimes one feels happy, sometimes one feels euphoric, ecstatic. A man deprived of all social relationships, isolated in total comfort, supplied with every need, moves through all the moods that you move through in relationship. That means that something comes from within, and you hang it on somebody else. That is just a rationalization.

You feel good, you feel bad, and these feelings are bubbling from your own unconsciousness, from your own past. Nobody is responsible except you. Nobody can make you angry, and nobody can make you happy. You become happy on your own, you become angry on your own, and you become sad on your own. Unless you realize this, you will always remain a slave.

> The mastery of one's self comes when one realizes, "I am absolutely responsible for whatsoever happens to me. Whatsoever happens, unconditionally—I am absolutely responsible."

In the beginning it will make you sad and depressed, because if you can throw the responsibility on the other, you feel good that you are not in the wrong. What can you do when the wife is behaving in such a nasty way? You have to be angry. But remember well, the wife is behaving nastily because of her own inner mechanisms. She's not nasty to you. If you were not there, she would be nasty to the child. If the child were not there, she would be nasty to the dishes; she would have thrown them on the floor. She would have broken the radio. She had to do something; nastiness was coming up. It was just coincidence that you were found reading your newspaper and she became nasty to you. It was just coincidence that you were available in a wrong moment.

> You feel good, you feel bad, and these feelings are bubbling from your own unconsciousness, from your own past. Nobody is responsible except you. Nobody can make you angry, and nobody can make you happy.

You are angry, not because the wife is nasty—she may have supplied the situation, that's all. She may have given you a possibility to be angry, an excuse to be angry, but the anger was bubbling up. If the wife were not there, you would have been angry all the same—with something else, with some idea, but anger had to be there. It was something that was coming from your own unconscious.

Everybody is responsible, totally responsible, for his own being and behavior. In the beginning it will make you depressed that you are responsible, because you have always thought that you want to be happy—so how can you be responsible for your unhappiness? You always desire blissfulness, so how can you be angry on your own? And because of this you throw the responsibility on the other.

If you go on throwing responsibility on the other, remember that you will always remain a slave because nobody can change the other. How can you change the other? Has anybody ever changed the other? One of the most unfulfilled wishes in the world is to change the other. Nobody has ever done that, it is impossible because the other exists in his own right—you cannot change him. You go on throwing responsibility on the other, but you cannot change the other. And because you throw the responsibility on the other, you will never see that the basic responsibility is yours. The basic change is needed there inside you.

This is how you are trapped: if you start thinking that you are responsible for all your actions, for all your moods, in the beginning a depression will take over. But if you can pass through that depression, soon you will feel light because now you are freed from the other. Now you can work on your own. You can be free, you can be happy. Even if the whole world is unhappy and unfree, it makes no difference. And the first freedom is to stop throwing responsibility on the other, the first freedom is to know that you are responsible. Then many things become immediately possible.

If you go on throwing responsibility on the other, remember that

> If you go on throwing responsibility on the other, remember that you will always remain a slave because nobody can change the other. How can you change the other? Has anybody ever changed the other?

you will always remain a slave because nobody can change the other. How can you change the other? Has anybody ever changed the other? Whatsoever happens to you—you feel sad, just close your eyes and watch your sadness—follow where it leads, go deeper into it. Soon you will come to the cause. Maybe you will have to travel long, because this whole life is involved; and not only this life but many other lives are involved. You will find many wounds in you, which hurt, and because of those wounds you feel sad—they are sad; those wounds have not gone dry yet; they are alive. The method of going back to the source, from the effect to the cause, will heal them. How does it heal? Why does it heal? What is the phenomenon implied in it?

Whenever you go backward, the first thing you drop is throwing the responsibility on others, because if you throw the responsibility on the other, you go outward. Then the whole process is wrong, you try to find the cause in the other: "Why is the wife nasty?" Then the "why" goes on penetrating into the wife's behavior. You have missed the first step and then the whole process will be wrong.

"Why am I unhappy? Why am I angry?"—close the eyes and let it be a deep meditation. Lie down on the floor, close the eyes, relax the body, and feel why you are angry. Just forget the wife; that is an excuse—A, B, C, D, whatsoever, forget the excuse. Just go deeper into yourself, penetrate the anger. Use anger itself as a river; into the anger you flow and the anger will take you inward. You will find subtle wounds in you. The wife looked nasty because she touched a subtle wound in you, something that hurts. You have always thought that you are not beautiful, your face is ugly, and there is a wound inside. When the wife is nasty, she will make you aware of your face. She will say, "Go and look in the mirror!"—something hurts. You have been unfaithful to the wife, and when she wants to be nasty, she will bring it up again: "Why were you laughing with that woman? Why were you sitting with that woman so happily?"—a wound is touched. You have been unfaithful, you feel guilty; the wound is alive.

You close the eyes, feel the anger, let it arise in its totality so that you can see it completely, what it is. Then let that energy help you to move toward the past, because the anger is coming from the past. It cannot come from the future, of course. The future has not yet come into being. It is not coming from the present. This is the whole standpoint of karma: it cannot come from the future because the future is not yet; it cannot come from the present because you don't know at all what the present is. The present is known only by the awakened ones. You live only in the past, so it must be coming from somewhere else in your past. The wound must be somewhere in your memories. Go back. There may not be one wound, there may be many—small, big. Go deeper and find the first wound, the original source of all anger. You will be able to find it if you try, because it is already there. It is there; all your past is still there. It is like a film, rolled and waiting inside. You unroll it, you start looking at the film. This is the process of going backward to the root cause. And this is the beauty of the process: if you can consciously go backward, if you can consciously feel a wound, the wound is immediately healed.

Why is it healed?—because a wound is created by unconsciousness, unawareness. A wound is part of ignorance, sleep. When you consciously go backward and look at the wound, consciousness is a healing force. In the past, when the wound happened, it happened in unconsciousness. You were angry, you were possessed by anger, you did something. You killed a man and you have been hiding the fact from the world. You can hide it from the police, you can hide it from the court and the law, but how can you hide it from yourself?—you know, it hurts. And whenever somebody gives you an opportunity to be angry, you become afraid because it could happen again, you could kill the wife. Go back, because at that moment when you murdered a man or you behaved in an angry and mad way, you were unconscious. In the unconscious those wounds have been preserved. Now go consciously.

Going back means going consciously to things that you have

> You need space—the past is so much inside, a junkyard of dead things, there is no space for the present to enter. That junkyard goes on dreaming about the future, so half the place is filled with that which is no more and half the place is filled with that which is not yet. And the present?—it simply waits outside the door.

done in unconsciousness. Go back—just the light of consciousness heals; it is a healing force. Whatsoever you can make conscious will be healed, and then it will hurt no more.

A man who goes backward releases the past. Then the past is no longer functioning, then the past has no more grip on him and the past is finished. The past has no place in his being. And when the past has no place in your being, you are available to the present, never before it.

You need space—the past is so much inside, a junkyard of dead things, there is no space for the present to enter. That junkyard goes on dreaming about the future, so half the place is filled with that which is no more and half the place is filled with that which is not yet. And the present?—it simply waits outside the door. That's why the present is nothing but a passage, a passage from the past to the future, just a momentary passage.

Be finished with the past—unless you are finished with the past, you are living a ghost life. Your life is not true, it is not existential. The past lives through you, the dead goes on haunting you. Go backward—whenever you have an opportunity, whenever something happens in you. Happiness, unhappiness, sadness, anger, jealousy—close the eyes and go backward. Soon you will become efficient in traveling backward. Soon you will be able to go back in time, and then many wounds will open. When those wounds open inside you, don't start doing anything. There is no need to *do*. You simply watch, look, observe. The wound is there—you simply watch, give your watching energy to the wound, look at it. Look at it without any judgment—because if you judge, if you say, "This is bad, this should not be so," the wound will close again. Then it will have to hide. Whenever you condemn, then the mind tries to hide things. That's how the conscious and unconscious are created. Otherwise, mind is one; there is no need for any division. But you condemn—then the mind has to divide and put things in the dark, in the basement, so you cannot see them and then there is no need to condemn.

Don't condemn, don't appreciate. You simply be a witness, an unattached observer. Don't deny. Don't say, "This is not good," because that is a denial and you have started suppressing.

Be detached. Just watch and look. Look with compassion and the healing will happen.

> Whenever you condemn, then the mind tries to hide things. That's how the conscious and unconscious are created. Otherwise, mind is one, there is no need for any division. But you condemn—then the mind has to divide and put things in the dark, in the basement, so you cannot see them.

Don't ask me why it happens, because it is a natural phenomenon—it is just as at a hundred degrees centigrade, water boils. You never ask, "Why not at ninety-nine degrees?" Nobody can answer that. It simply happens that at a hundred degrees water boils. There is no question, and the question is irrelevant. If it boiled at ninety-nine degrees, you would ask why. If it boiled at ninety-eight, you would ask why. It is simply natural that at a hundred degrees water boils.

The same is true of the inner nature. When a detached, compassionate consciousness comes to a wound, the wound disappears—evaporates. There is no why to it. It is simply natural, it is how it is, it is how it happens. When I say this, I say it from experience. Try it and the experience is possible for you also. This is the way.

AWARENESS IN ACTION

A man who is asleep cannot be total in anything. You are eating, you are not totally there; you are thinking a thousand and one things, you are dreaming a thousand and one dreams, you are just stuffing yourself mechanically. You may be making love to your woman or to your man, and you are not totally there. You may be thinking of other women, making love to your wife and thinking of some other woman. Or you may be thinking of the market, or of the prices of things that you want to purchase, or of a car, or of a house, or of a thousand and one things—and you are making love mechanically.

Be total in your acts, and <u>if you are total, you have to be aware; nobody can be total without being aware.</u> Being total means no other thinking. If you are eating, you are simply eating; you are totally here now. The eating is all: you are not just stuffing yourself, you are enjoying it. <u>Body, mind, soul, all are in tune</u> while you are eating and there is a harmony, a deep rhythm, in all three layers of your being. Then eating becomes meditation, walking becomes meditation, chopping wood becomes meditation, carrying water from the well becomes meditation, cooking food becomes meditation. <u>Small things are transformed: they become luminous acts.</u>

START FROM THE CENTER

One thing to be understood is that silence is not part of mind. So whenever we say, "He has a silent mind," it is nonsense. A mind can never be silent. The very being of mind is antisilence. Mind is sound, not silence. If a person is really silent, then we must say that he has no mind.

> Whenever we say, "He has a silent mind," it is nonsense. A mind can never be silent. The very being of mind is antisilence. Mind is sound, not silence. If a person is really silent, then we must say that he has no mind.

A "silent mind" is a contradiction in terms. If mind is there, it cannot be silent; and if it is silent, it is no more. That is why Zen monks use the term *no-mind,* never *silent mind.* No-mind is silence—and the moment there is no-mind you cannot feel your body, because mind is the passage through which body is felt. If there is no-mind, you cannot feel that you are a body; the body disappears from consciousness. There is neither mind nor body—only pure existence. That pure existence is indicated by silence.

How to attain to this silence? How to be in this silence? Whatsoever you can do will be useless; that is the greatest problem. For a seeker of silence, this is the greatest problem because whatsoever you can do will lead nowhere—because doing is not relevant. You can sit in a particular posture—that is your doing. You must have seen Buddha's posture; you can sit in Buddha's posture—that will be a doing. For Buddha himself this posture happened. It was not a cause for his silence; rather, it was a by-product.

When the mind is not, when the being is totally silent, the body follows like a shadow. The body takes a particular posture—the most relaxed possible, the most passive possible. But you cannot do it the other way around. You cannot take a posture first and then make silence follow. Because we see a Buddha sitting in a particular posture, we think that if this posture is followed, then the inner silence will follow. This is a wrong sequence. For Buddha the inner phenomenon happened first, and then this posture followed.

Look at it through your own experience: when you get angry, the body takes a particular posture. Your eyes become bloodred, your face takes a particular expression. Anger is inside and then the body follows—not only outwardly, inwardly also, the whole chemistry of the body changes. Your blood runs fast, you breathe in a different way, you are ready to fight or take flight. But anger happens first, then the body follows.

Start from the other pole: make your eyes red, create fast breathing, do whatever you feel is done by the body when anger is there. You can act, but you cannot create anger inside. An actor is doing the same every moment. When he is acting a role of love, he is doing whatever is done by the body when love happens inside, but there is no love. The actor may be doing better than you, but love will not follow. He will be more apparently angry than you are in real anger, but it is just false. Nothing is happening inside.

> When the mind is not, when the being is totally silent, the body follows like a shadow. The body takes a particular posture—the most relaxed possible, the most passive possible. But you cannot do it the other way around. You cannot take a posture first and then make silence follow.

Whenever you start from without, you will create a false state. The real always happens first in the center, and then the waves reach to the periphery.

The innermost center is in silence. Start from there.

IT IS ONLY OUT OF SILENCE THAT ACTION ARISES. If you are not silent—if you don't know how to sit silently, or stand silently in deep meditation—whatsoever you go on doing is *reaction,* not action. You react. Somebody insults you, pushes a button, and you react. You are angry, you jump on him—and you call it action? It is not action, mind you, it is reaction. He is the manipulator and you are the manipulated. He has pushed a button and you have functioned like a machine. Just as you push a button and the light goes on, and you push the button and the light goes off—that's what people are doing to you. They put you on, they put you off.

Somebody comes and praises you and puffs up your ego, and you feel so great. And then somebody comes and punctures you, and you are simply flat on the ground. You are not your own master. Anybody can insult you and make you sad, angry, irritated, annoyed, violent, mad. And anybody can praise you and make you feel at the heights, can make you feel that you are the greatest, that Alexander the Great was nothing compared to you. And you act according to others' manipulations. This is not real action.

Buddha was passing through a village and the people came and they insulted him. And they used all the insulting words that they could use—

> If you are not silent—if you don't know how to sit silently, or stand silently in deep meditation—whatsoever you go on doing is *reaction,* not action. You react. Somebody insults you, pushes a button, and you react.

all the four-letter words that they knew. Buddha stood there, listened silently, attentively, and then said, "Thank you for coming to me, but I am in a hurry. I have to reach the next village, people will be waiting for me there. I cannot devote more time to you today, but tomorrow, coming back, I will have more time. You can gather again, and tomorrow if something is left that you wanted to say and have not been able to say, you can say it to me. But today, excuse me."

Those people could not believe their ears, their eyes: this man has remained utterly unaffected, undistracted. One of them asked, "Have you not heard us? We have been abusing you like anything, and you have not even answered!"

Buddha said, "If you wanted an answer, then you have come too late. You should have come ten years ago, then I would have answered you. But for these ten years I have stopped being manipulated by others. I am no longer a slave, I am my own master. I act according to myself, not according to anybody else. I act according to my inner need. You cannot force me to do anything. It's perfectly good—you wanted to abuse me, you abused me. Feel fulfilled; you have done your work perfectly well. But as far as I am concerned, I don't take your insults, and unless I take them, they are meaningless."

When somebody insults you, you have to become a receiver; you have to accept what he says, only then can you react. But if you don't accept, if you simply remain detached, if you keep the distance, if you remain cool, what can he do?

> When somebody insults you, you have to become a receiver; you have to accept what he says, only then can you react. But if you don't accept, if you simply remain detached, if you keep the distance, if you remain cool, what can he do?

> ☙
>
> Watching should
> lead you into action,
> a new kind of action.
> A new quality is
> brought to action.
> You watch, you are
> utterly quiet and
> silent. You see what
> the situation is, and
> out of that seeing you
> respond. The man of
> awareness responds, he
> is *responsible*—
> literally!

Buddha said, "Somebody can throw a burning torch into the river. It will remain alight till it reaches the river. The moment it falls into the river, all fire is gone—the river cools it. I have become a river. You throw abuses at me—they are fire when you throw them, but the moment they reach me, in my coolness their fire is lost. They no longer hurt. You throw thorns—falling in my silence, they become flowers. I act out of my own intrinsic nature."

This is spontaneity.

The man of awareness, understanding, acts. The man who is unaware, unconscious, mechanical, robotlike, reacts.

And it is not that the man of awareness simply watches—watching is one aspect of his being. He does not act without watching. But don't misunderstand—the whole of India, for example, has been misunderstanding people like Buddha; hence the whole country has become inactive. Thinking that all the great masters say, "Sit silently," the country became lazy, lousy. The country lost energy, vitality, life. It became utterly dull, unintelligent, because intelligence becomes sharpened only when you act.

And when you act moment to moment out of your awareness and watchfulness, great intelligence arises. You start shining, glowing, you become luminous. But it happens through two things: watching, and action out of that watching. If watching becomes inaction, you are committing suicide.

Watching should lead you into action, a new kind of action. A new quality is brought to action. You watch, you are utterly quiet and silent. You see what the situation is, and out of that seeing you respond. The man of awareness responds, he is *responsible*—literally! He is responsive, he does not react. His action is born out of his awareness, not out of your manipulation; that is the difference. Hence, there is no incompatibility between watching and spontaneity. Watching is the beginning of spontaneity; spontaneity is the fulfillment of watching.

The real man of understanding acts—acts tremendously, acts totally, but he acts in the moment, out of his consciousness. He is like a mirror. The ordinary man, the unconscious man, is not like a mirror, he is like a photo plate. What is the difference between a mirror and a photo plate? A photo plate, once exposed, becomes useless. It receives the impression, becomes impressed by it—it carries the picture. But remember, the picture is not reality—the reality goes on growing. You can go into the garden and you can take a picture of a rosebush. Tomorrow the picture will be the same, the day after tomorrow the picture will also be the same. Go again and see the rosebush—it is no longer the same. The roses have gone, or new roses have arrived. A thousand and one things have happened.

Life is never static, it goes on changing. Your mind functions like a camera, it goes on collecting pictures—it is an album. And then out of those pictures you go on reacting. Hence, you are never true to life, because whatsoever you do is wrong. *Whatever* you do, I say, is wrong. It never fits.

A woman was showing the family album to her child, and they came across a picture of a beautiful man—thick hair, beard, very young, very alive. The boy asked, "Mommy, who is this man?"

And the woman said, "Can't you recognize him? He is your daddy!"

The boy looked puzzled and said, "If he is my daddy, then who is that bald man who lives with us?"

A picture is static. It remains as it is, it never changes.

The unconscious mind functions like a camera, it functions like a photo plate. The watchful mind, the meditative mind, functions like a mirror. It catches no impression; it remains utterly empty, always empty. So whatsoever comes in front of the mirror, it is reflected. If you are standing before the mirror, it reflects you. If you are gone, don't say that the mirror betrays you. The mirror is simply a mirror. When you are gone, it no longer reflects you; it has no obligation to reflect you anymore. Now somebody else is facing it—it reflects somebody else. If nobody is there, it reflects nothing. It is always true to life.

> The unconscious mind functions like a camera, it functions like a photo plate. The watchful mind, the meditative mind, functions like a mirror. It catches no impression, it remains utterly empty, always empty. So whatsoever comes in front of the mirror, it is reflected.

The photo plate is never true to life. Even if your photo is taken right now, by the time the photographer has taken it out of the camera, you are no longer the same! Much water has already gone down the Ganges. You have grown, changed, you have become older. Maybe only one minute has passed, but one minute can be a great thing—you may be dead! Just one minute before, you were alive; after one minute, you may be dead. The picture will never die.

But in the mirror, if you are alive, you are alive; if you are dead, you are dead.

Learn sitting silently—become a

mirror. Silence makes a mirror out of your consciousness, and then you function moment to moment. You reflect life. You don't carry an album within your head. Then your eyes are clear and innocent, you have clarity, you have vision, and you are never untrue to life.

This is authentic living.

BE SPONTANEOUS

When you act, you are always acting through the past. You are acting out of experience that you have accumulated, you are acting out of the conclusions that you have arrived at in the past—how can you be spontaneous?

The past dominates, and because of the past you cannot even see the present. Your eyes are so full of the past, the smoke of the past is so great, that seeing is impossible. You cannot see! You are almost completely blind—blind because of the smoke, blind because of the past conclusions, blind because of knowledge.

The knowledgeable man is the most blind man in the world. Because he functions out of his knowledge, he does not see what the case is. He simply goes on functioning mechanically. He has learned something; it has become a ready-made mechanism in him and he acts out of it.

There is a famous story:

There were two temples in Japan, both enemies to each other, as temples have always been down the ages. The priests were so antagonistic that they had stopped even looking at each other. If they came across each other on the road, they would not look at each other. If they came across each other on the road, they stopped talking; for centuries those two temples and their priests had not talked.

But each priest had a small boy—to serve him, just for

> The knowledgeable man is the most blind man in the world. Because he functions out of his knowledge, he does not see what the case is. He simply goes on functioning mechanically. He has learned something, it has become a ready-made mechanism in him and he acts out of it.

running errands. Both the priests were afraid that boys will after all be boys, and they might start becoming friends to each other.

The one priest said to his boy, "Remember, the other temple is our enemy. Never talk to the boy of the other temple. They are dangerous people—avoid them as one avoids a disease. As one avoids the plague, avoid them!"

The boy was interested . . . because he used to get tired of listening to great sermons. He could not understand them. Strange scriptures were read, he could not understand the language; great, ultimate problems were discussed. There was nobody to play with, nobody even to talk with. And when he was told, "Don't talk to the boy of the other temple," great temptation arose in him. That's how temptation arises. That day he could not avoid talking to the other boy. When he saw him on the road, he asked him, "Where are you going?"

The other boy was a little philosophical; listening to great philosophy he had become philosophical. He said, "Going? There is nobody who comes and goes! It is happening—wherever the wind takes me." He had heard the master say many times that that's how a buddha lives, like a dead leaf, wherever the wind takes it, it goes. So the boy said, "I am not! There is no doer, so how can I go? What nonsense are you talking? I am a dead leaf. Wherever the wind takes me. . . ."

The other boy was struck dumb. He could not even answer. He could not find anything to say. He was really embarrassed, ashamed, and felt, "My master was right not to talk with these people—these *are* dangerous people. What kind of talk is this? I had asked a simple question: 'Where are you going?' In fact I already knew where he was going, because we were both going to purchase vegetables in the market. A simple answer would have done."

The boy went back, told his master, "I am sorry, excuse me. You had prohibited me, but I didn't listen to you. In fact, because of your prohibition I was tempted. This is the first time I have talked to those dangerous people. I just asked a simple question, 'Where are you going?' and he started saying strange things: 'There is no going, no coming. Who comes? Who goes? I am utter emptiness,' he was saying, 'just a dead leaf in the wind. And wherever the wind takes me . . .' "

The master said, "I told you! Now, tomorrow stand in the same place, and when he comes, ask him again, 'Where are you going?' And when he says these things, you simply say, 'That's true. Yes, you are a dead leaf, so am I. But when the wind is not blowing, where are you going? Then where can you go?' Just say that, and that will embarrass him—and he has to be embarrassed, he has to be defeated. We have been constantly quarreling, and those people have not been able to defeat us in any debate. So tomorrow it has to be done!"

The boy got up early, prepared his answer, repeated it many times before he went. Then he stood in the place where the boy would cross the road, repeated again and again, prepared himself, and then he saw the boy coming. He said, "Okay, now!"

The boy came. The first boy asked, "Where are you going?" And he was hoping that now the opportunity would come.

But the boy said, "Wherever the legs will take me." No mention of wind, no talk of nothingness, no question of the nondoer . . . Now what to do? His whole ready-made answer looked absurd. Now to talk about the wind would be irrelevant. Again crestfallen, now really ashamed that he was simply stupid, thinking, "This boy certainly knows some strange things. Now he says, 'Wherever the legs take me.' "

The boy went back to the master. The master said, "I had told you not to talk with those people! They are dangerous, this is our centuries-long experience. But now something has to be done. So tomorrow you ask again, 'Where are you going?' and when he says, 'Wherever my legs take me,' tell him, 'If you had no legs, then . . . ?' He has to be silenced one way or another."

So the next day the boy asked again, "Where are you going?" and waited.

And the boy said, "I am going to the market to fetch vegetables."

Man ordinarily functions out of the past—and life goes on changing. Life has no obligation to fit with your conclusions. That's why life is confusing—confusing to the knowledgeable person. He has all the ready-made answers, the Bhagavad Gita, the Holy Koran, the Bible, the Vedas. He has everything crammed, he knows all the answers. But life never raises the same question again; hence the knowledgeable person always falls short.

BE DECISIVE

Mind is never decisive. It is not a question of one person's mind or another's; mind is indecisiveness. The functioning of the mind is to waver between two polar opposites and try to find which is the right way. It is as if by closing your eyes you are trying to find the door. Certainly you will feel yourself hanging between the two—to go this way or that; you will be always in a condition of either/or. That's the nature of mind.

One great Danish philosopher was Søren Kierkegaard. He wrote a book, *Either/Or*. It was his own life's experience—he could never decide about anything! Everything was always such that if he was deciding *this* way, then *that* way seemed to be right. If he was deciding *that* way, then *this* way seemed to be right. He remained unmarried, although a woman was very much in love with him and had asked him to marry. But he said, "I will have to think about it—marriage is a big thing, and I cannot say yes or no immediately." And he died with the question, without getting married.

He lived only forty-two years, and he was continually arguing, discussing, but he found no answer that could be said to be the ultimate answer, which had not its equal opposite. He could never become a professor. He had filled out the application, he had all the best qualifications possible—he had many books to his credit, of such immense importance that even after a century they are still contemporary, not old, not out-of-date. He filled out the application but could not sign it—because "either/or" . . . whether to join the university or not? The application was found when he died, in the small room where he lived.

He would stop at a crossroads to decide to go this way or to go that way, for hours . . . ! The whole of Copenhagen became aware of this man's strangeness, and children nicknamed him Either/Or, so urchins would be following him, shouting, "Either/Or!" wherever he would go. Seeing the situation, his father liquidated all his businesses before he died, collected all the money, deposited it into an account, and arranged that every month on the first day of the month, Kierkegaard should receive so much money. So for his whole life he could at least survive . . . and you will be surprised: the day he was coming home, after taking out the last installment of the money on the first day of the month—the money was finished— he fell on the street and died. With the last installment! That was the right thing to do. What else to do?—because after this month, what could he do?

He was writing books but was not decisive about whether to publish them or not; he left many of his books unpublished. They are of tremendous value. Each book has a great penetration into things. On each subject he has written, he has gone to the very roots, to every minute detail . . . a genius, but a genius of the mind.

With the mind, that is the problem—and the better mind you have, the more will be the problem. Lesser minds don't come across that problem so much. It is the mind of the genius that is stuck between two polarities and cannot choose. And then he feels in a limbo.

What I have been telling you is that it is the nature of the mind to be in a limbo. It is the nature of the mind to be in the middle of polar opposites. Unless you move away from the mind and become a witness to all the games of the mind, you will never be decisive. Even if you sometimes decide—in spite of the mind—you will repent, because the other half that you have not decided for is going to haunt you: perhaps that was right and what you have chosen is wrong. And now there is no way to know. Perhaps the choice that you had left aside was better. But even if you had chosen it, the situation would not have been different. Then this choice, which would have been left aside, would haunt you.

Mind is basically the beginning of madness. And if you are too much in it, it will drive you mad.

In my village I used to live opposite a goldsmith. I used to sit just in front of his house, and I became aware that he had a curious habit: he would lock his shop, then pull the lock two, three times to see whether it was really locked. One day I was coming from the river and he had just locked his shop and was going home. I said, "But you have not checked!"

He said, "What?"

I said, "You have not checked the lock!" He had checked it—I had seen him pulling on it three times, but now I had created a suspicion, and the mind is always ready . . .

So he said to me, "Perhaps I forgot—I must go back." He went back and checked the lock again. That became my joy—wherever he would go . . . in the market he would be purchasing vegetables, and I would go there and say, "What are you doing here? You have left the lock unchecked!"

> It is the nature of the mind to be in the middle of polar opposites. Unless you move away from the mind and become a witness to all the games of the mind, you will never be decisive.

He would drop his vegetables and say, "I will be coming back; first I have to go and check the lock." Even at the railway station—he was purchasing a ticket to go somewhere, and I went and told him, "What are you doing? The lock!"

He said, "My God, have I not checked it?"

I said, "No!"

He said, "Now it is impossible to go." He returned his ticket, went home, and checked the lock. But then it was too late to go back to the station—the train had already gone. And he trusted me because I was always sitting in front of his house.

Slowly it became known to everybody, so wherever he would go, people would say, "Where are you going? Have you checked your lock?"

Finally he became angry with me. He said, "You must be spreading it, because wherever I go, everybody is talking about the lock."

I said, "Then don't listen to them. Let them say whatsoever they want."

He said, "What do you mean, don't listen to them! If they are right, then I am lost forever. I cannot take that chance. So knowing perfectly well that the man may be lying, I have to come back compulsively to check the lock. I know somewhere that I have checked it, but who can be certain?"

Mind has no certainty about anything.

> Be aware of the mind— its bright side, its dark side, its right, its wrong. Whatever polarity it is, you just be aware of it. Two things will come out of that awareness: one, that you are not the mind, and second, that awareness has a decisiveness that mind never has.

If you are between the two polarities of the mind, in a limbo—always to do or not to do, you will go crazy. You *are* crazy! Before it happens, jump out and have a look from the outside at the mind.

Be aware of the mind—its bright side, its dark side, its right, its wrong. Whatever polarity it is, you just be aware of it. Two things will come out of that awareness: first, that you are not the mind, and second, that awareness has a decisiveness that mind never has.

Mind is basically indecisive, and awareness is basically decisive. So any act out of awareness is total, full, without repentance.

I have never in my life thought again about anything, whether something else would have been better. I have never repented. I have never thought that I have committed any mistake, because there is nobody else who has been left to say these things. I have been acting out of my awareness—that is my whole being. Now whatever happens is all that is possible. The world may call it right or wrong, that is their business, but it is not my problem.

So awareness will take you out of the limbo. Rather than hanging between these two polarities of the mind, you will jump beyond both, and you will be able to see that those polarities are polarities only if you are in the mind. If you are outside it, you will be surprised that they are two sides of the same coin—there was no question of decision.

With awareness you have the clarity, totality, the let-go—existence decides within you. You don't have to think about what is right and wrong. Existence takes your hand in its hand, and you are moving in a relaxed way. That's the only way, the right way. And that is the only way you can be sane; otherwise you will remain muddled.

Now, Søren Kierkegaard is a great mind, but being a Christian, he had no concept of awareness. He can think, and think very deeply, but he cannot just be silent and watch. That poor fellow had never heard about anything like watching, witnessing, awareness. Thinking was all that he had heard about, and he had put his whole genius into thinking. He had produced great books, but he could not produce a great life for himself. He lived in utter misery.

COMPLETE EACH MOMENT

Why is dreaming needed? You wanted to kill someone and you have not killed—you will kill him in your dream. That will relax your mind. In the morning you will be fresh—you have killed. I am not saying to go and kill so that you will not need any dream! But remember this: if you want to kill someone, close your room, meditate on the killing, and consciously kill him. When I say "kill him," I mean kill a pillow; make an effigy and kill it. That conscious effort, that conscious meditation, will give you much insight into yourself.

Remember one thing: make every moment complete. Live every moment as if there is no other moment to come. Then only will you complete it. Know that death can occur at any moment. This may be the last. Feel that "if I have to do something, I must do it here and now, *completely!*"

> ≈
>
> Remember one thing: make every moment complete. Live every moment as if there is no other moment to come. Then only will you complete it. Know that death can occur at any moment. This may be the last.

I have heard a story about a Greek general. The king was somehow against him. There was a court conspiracy, and it was the general's birthday. He was celebrating it with his friends. Suddenly, in the afternoon, the king's manager came and said to the general, "Excuse me, it is hard to tell you, but the king has decided that this evening by six o'clock you are to be hanged. So be ready by six o'clock."

Friends were there; music was playing. There was drinking, eating, and dancing. It was his birthday. This message changed the whole atmosphere. Everybody became sad. But the general said, "Now do not be sad, because this is going to be the last part of my life. So let us complete the dance we were dancing and let us complete the feast we were having. I have no possibility now, so we cannot make it complete in the future. And do not send me off in this sad atmosphere; otherwise my mind will long for life again and again, and the stopped music and the halted festivity will become a burden on my mind. So let us complete it. Now is no time to stop it."

Because of him they danced, but it was difficult. He alone danced more vigorously; he alone became more festive—but the whole group was simply not there. His wife was weeping but he continued to dance, he continued to talk with his friends. And he was so happy that the messenger went back to the king and said, "That man is rare. He has heard the message but he is not sad. And he has taken it in a very different way—absolutely inconceivable. He is laughing and dancing and he is festive, and he says that because these moments are his last and there is no future now, he cannot waste them—he must live them."

The king himself went to see what was happening there. Everyone was sad, weeping. Only the general was dancing, drinking, singing. The king asked, "What are you doing?"

The general said, "This has been my life principle—to be aware continuously that death is possible any moment. Because of this principle I have lived every moment as much as was possible. But of course you have made it so clear today. I am grateful because until now I was only *thinking* that death is possible any moment. It was just a thinking. Somewhere, lurking behind, was the thought that it was not going to be just the next moment. The future was there. But you dropped the future completely for me. This evening is the last. Life now is so short, I cannot postpone it."

The king was so happy, he became a disciple to this man. He said, "Teach me! This is the alchemy. This is how life should be lived; this is the art. I am not going to hang you, but be my teacher. Teach me how to live in the moment."

We are postponing. That postponing becomes an inner dialogue, an inner monologue. Do not postpone. Live right here and now. And the more you live in the present, the less you will

> Postponing becomes an inner dialogue, an inner monologue. Do not postpone. Live right here and now. And the more you live in the present, the less you will need this constant "minding," this constant thinking.

> That which you have missed, you go on thinking you will catch somewhere in the future. You are not going to catch it! This constant tension between past and future, this constant missing of the present, is the inner noise.

need this constant "minding," this constant thinking. The less you will need it! It is there because of postponing, and we go on postponing everything. We always live in the tomorrow, which never comes and which cannot come; it is impossible. That which comes is always today, and we go on sacrificing today for tomorrow, which is nowhere. Then the mind goes on thinking of the past, which you have destroyed, which you have sacrificed for something that has not come. And then it goes on postponing for further tomorrows.

That which you have missed, you go on thinking you will catch somewhere in the future. You are not going to catch it! This constant tension between past and future, this constant missing of the present, is the inner noise. Unless it stops, you cannot fall into silence. So the first thing: try to be total in every moment.

The second thing: your mind is so noisy because you always go on thinking that others are creating it, that you are not responsible. So you go on thinking that in a better world—with a better wife, with a better husband, with better children, with a better house, in a better locality—everything will be good and you will be silent. You think you are not silent because everything around is wrong, so how can you be?

If you think in this way, if this is your logic, then that better world is never going to come. Everywhere this is the world, everywhere these are the neighbors, and everywhere these are the wives and these are the husbands and these are the children. You can create an illusion that somewhere heaven exists, but everywhere it is hell. With this type of mind, everywhere is hell. This *mind* is hell.

One day Mulla Nasruddin and his wife came home to their house, late in the night. The house had been burglarized, so the wife began to scream and cry. Then she said to Mulla, "You are at fault! Why didn't you check the lock before we left?"

By then the whole neighborhood had come around. It was such a sensation—Mulla's house had been burglarized! Everyone joined in the chant. One neighbor said, "I was always expecting it. Why didn't you expect it before? You are so careless!" The second said, "Your windows were open. Why didn't you close them before you left the house?" The third one said, "Your locks appear to be faulty. Why didn't you replace them?" And everyone was pouring faults on Mulla Nasruddin.

Then he said, "One minute please! I am not at fault."

So the whole neighborhood said in a chorus, "Then who do you think is at fault if you are not?"

Mulla said, "What about the thief?"

The mind goes on throwing the blame on someone else. The wife throws it on Mulla Nasruddin, the whole neighborhood on Mulla Nasruddin, and the poor man cannot throw it on anyone present, so he says, "What about the thief?"

We go on throwing the blame on others. This gives you an illusory feeling that you are not wrong. Someone else somewhere is wrong—X–Y–Z. And this attitude is one of the basic attitudes of our mind. In everything someone else is wrong, and whenever we can find a scapegoat, we are at ease; then the burden is thrown.

For a seeker, this mind is of no help; it is a hindrance. This mind is the hindrance. We must realize that whatever the situation is, whatever the case is with you, *you* are responsible and no one else. If you are responsible, then something is possible. If someone else is responsible, then nothing is possible.

This is a basic conflict between the religious mind and the irreligious mind. The irreligious mind always thinks that something else is responsible—change the society, change the circumstances, change economic conditions, change the political situation, change *something,* and everything will be okay. We have changed everything so many times, and nothing is okay. The religious mind says that whatsoever the situation, if this is your mind, then you will be in hell, you will be in misery. You won't be able to attain silence.

Put the responsibility on yourself. Be responsible because then something can be done. You can only do something with yourself. You cannot change anyone else in this world, you can only change yourself. That is the only revolution possible. The only transformation possible is one's own. But that can be considered only when we feel that we are responsible.

STOP TRYING TO BE GOOD

The only sin is unawareness, and the only virtue is awareness. That which cannot be done without unawareness is sin. That which can only be done through awareness is virtue. It is impossible to murder if you are aware; it is impossible to be violent at all—if you are aware. It is impossible to rape, to steal, to torture—these are impossibilities if awareness is there. It is only when unawareness prevails that, in the darkness of unawareness, all kinds of enemies enter you.

Buddha has said: If the light is on in a house, thieves avoid it; and if the watchman is awake, thieves will not even try. And if the people are walking and talking inside, and the house has not yet fallen into sleep, there is no possibility for thieves to enter or even to think about it.

Exactly the same is the case with you: you are a house without any light. The ordinary state of man is that of a mechanical functioning: *Homo mechanicus*. Only in name are you human—otherwise, just a trained, skillful machine, and whatsoever you do is going to be wrong. And remember, I am saying *whatsoever* you do—even your virtues will not be virtues if you are unaware. How can you be virtuous when you are unaware? Behind your virtue will come a great, enormous ego—it is bound to be so.

Even your saintliness, practiced, cultivated with great labor and effort, is futile. Because it will not bring simplicity and it will not bring humbleness, and it will not bring that great experience of the divine, which happens only when the ego has disappeared. You will live a respectable life as a saint, but as poor as everybody else—inwardly rotten, inwardly a meaningless existence. It is not life, it is only vegetating. Your sins will be sins, your virtues will also be sins. Your immorality will be immorality, your morality will also be immorality.

I don't teach morality, and I don't teach virtue—because I know that without awareness they are just pretensions, hypocrisies. They make you phony. They don't liberate you, they can't liberate you. On the contrary, they imprison you.

Only one thing is enough: awareness is a master key. It unlocks all the locks of existence. Awareness means you live moment to moment, alert, conscious of yourself and conscious of

> How can you be virtuous when you are unaware? Behind your virtue will come a great, enormous ego—it is bound to be so. Even your saintliness, practiced, cultivated with great labor and effort, is futile. Because it will not bring simplicity and it will not bring humbleness.

all that is happening around you in a moment-to-moment response. You are like a mirror, you reflect—and you reflect so totally that out of that reflection whatsoever act is born is right because it fits, it is harmonious with existence. It does not really arise in *you*—you are not a *doer* of it. It arises in the total context—the situation, you and all, are involved in it. Out of that wholeness the act is born—it is not your act, you have not decided to do it that way. It is not your decision, it is not your thought, it is not your character. You are not doing it, you are only allowing it to happen.

> ❧
>
> I don't teach morality, and I don't teach virtue—because I know that without awareness they are just pretensions, hypocrisies. They make you phony. They don't liberate you, they can't liberate you. On the contrary, they imprison you.

It is just as if you are walking early in the morning, the sun has not risen, and you come across a snake on the path—there is no time to think. You can only reflect—there is no time to decide what to do and what not to do—you immediately jump! Note the word *immediately*—not even a single moment is lost; you immediately jump out of the way. Later on you can sit underneath a tree and think about it, what happened, how you did it, and you can pat your own back that you did well. But in fact you have not done it—it happened. It happened out of the total context. You, the snake, the danger of death, the effort of life to protect itself . . . and a thousand and one other things are involved in it. The total situation caused the act. You were just a medium.

Now, this act *fits*. You are not the doer of it. In the religious way we can say God has done it through you. That is only a religious way of speaking, that's all. The whole has acted through the part.

This is virtue. You will never repent for it. And this is really a freeing act. Once it has happened, it is finished. You are again free to act; you will not carry this action in your head. It will not become part of your psychological memory; it will not leave any wound in you. It was so spontaneous that it will not leave any trace. This act will never become a karma. This act will never leave any scratch on you. The act that becomes a karma is the act that is not really an act but a reaction—which comes from the past, from memory, from thinking. You are the decider, the chooser. It is not out of awareness but unawareness. Then it is all sin.

MY WHOLE MESSAGE IS THAT YOU NEED A CONSCIOUSNESS, NOT A CHARACTER. Consciousness is the real thing, character the false entity. Character is needed by those who don't have consciousness. If you have eyes, you don't need a walking stick to find your way, to grope your way around. If you can see, you don't ask others, "Where is the door?"

Character is needed because people are unconscious. Character is just a lubricant; it helps you to run your life in a smooth way. George Gurdjieff used to say character is like a buffer. Buffers are used in railway trains; between two compartments there are buffers. If something happens, these buffers prevent the compartments from clashing with each other. Or it is like springs: cars have springs so you can move smoothly. The springs go on absorbing the shocks; they are called shock absorbers. That's what character is: it is a shock absorber.

People are told to be humble. If you learn how to be humble, it is a shock absorber—by learning how to be humble you will be able to protect yourself against other people's egos. They will not hurt you so much; you are a humble man. If you are egoistic, you are bound to be hurt again and again—the ego is very sensitive—so

> Character is needed by those who don't have consciousness. If you have eyes, you don't need a walking stick to find your way, to grope your way around. If you can see, you don't ask others, "Where is the door?"

you cover up your ego with a blanket of humbleness. It helps, it gives you a kind of smoothness. But it does not transform you.

My work consists of transformation. This is an alchemical school; I want you to be transformed from unconsciousness into consciousness, from darkness into light. I cannot give you a character; I can only give you insight, awareness. I would like you to live moment to moment, not according to a set pattern given by me or given by the society, the church, the state. I would like you to live according to your own small light of awareness, according to your own consciousness.

Be responsive to each moment. Character means you have a certain ready-made answer for all the questions of life, so whenever a situation arises, you respond according to the set pattern. Because you respond according to the ready-made answer, it is not a true response, it is only a reaction. The man of character reacts, the man of consciousness responds: he takes the situation in, he reflects the reality as it is, and out of that reflection he acts. The man of character reacts, the man of consciousness acts. The man of character is mechanical; robotlike he functions. He has a computer in his mind, full of information; ask him anything and a ready-made answer rolls down from his computer.

A man of consciousness simply acts in the moment, not out of the past and out of memory. His response has a beauty, a naturalness, and his response is true to the situation. The man of character always falls short, because life is continuously changing; it is never the same.

And your answers are always the same, they never grow—they can't grow, they are dead.

You have been told a certain thing in your childhood; it has remained there. You have grown, life has changed, but that answer that was given by your parents or by your teachers or by your priests is still there. And if something happens, you will function according to the answer that was given to you fifty years before. And in fifty years so much water has gone down the Ganges; it is a totally different life.

Heraclitus says: <u>You cannot step in the same river twice</u>. And I say to you: You cannot step in the same river even once, the river is so fast flowing.

<u>Character is stagnant;</u> it is a dirty pool of water. Consciousness is a river.

That's why I don't give my people any code of conduct. I give them <u>eyes to see, a consciousness to reflect,</u> a <u>mirrorlike being</u> to be able to respond to any situation that arises. I don't give them detailed information about what to do and what not to do; I don't give them ten commandments. And if you start giving them commandments, then you cannot stop at ten, because life is far more complex.

In Buddhist scriptures there are thirty-three thousand rules for a Buddhist monk. Thirty-three thousand rules! For every possible situation that may ever arise, they have given a ready-made answer. But how are you going to remember thirty-three thousand

Character means you have a certain ready-made answer for all the questions of life, so whenever a situation arises, you respond according to the set pattern. Because you respond according to the ready-made answer, it is not a true response, it is only a reaction.

> ❧
>
> A man who is cunning enough to remember thirty-three thousand rules of conduct will be clever enough to find a way out, always; if he does not want to do a certain thing, he will find a way out. If he wants to do a certain thing, he will find a way out.

rules of conduct? And a man who is cunning enough to remember thirty-three thousand rules of conduct will be clever enough to find a way out, always; if he does not want to do a certain thing, he will find a way out. If he wants to do a certain thing, he will find a way out.

I have heard about a Christian saint: somebody hit him on his face, because just that day in his morning discourse he had said, "Jesus says if somebody slaps you on one cheek, give him the other." And the man wanted to try it, so he hit him, really hit him hard on one cheek. And the saint was really true, true to his word: he gave him the other cheek. But that man was also something: he hit even harder on the other cheek. Then he was surprised: the saint jumped on the man, started beating him so hard that the man said, "What are you doing? You are a saint, and just this morning you were saying that if somebody hits you on one cheek, give him the other."

The saint said, "Yes—but I don't have a third cheek. And Jesus stops there. Now I am free; now I will do what I want to do. Jesus has no more information about it."

It happened exactly like that in Jesus' life also. Once he told a disciple, "Forgive seven times." The disciple said "Okay." The way he said "Okay," Jesus became suspicious; he said, "Seventy-seven times I say."

The disciple was a little disturbed, but he said, "Okay—because numbers don't end at seventy-seven. What about seventy-eight? Then I am free, then I can do what I want to do!"

How many rules can you make for people? It is stupid, meaningless. That's how people are religious, and still they are not religious: they always find a way to get out of those rules of conduct and commandments. They can always find a way through the back door. And character can at the most give you only a skin-deep, pseudo mask—not even skin-deep: just scratch your saints a little bit and you will find the animal hidden behind. On the surface they look beautiful, but only on the surface.

I don't want you to be superficial; I want you to *really* change. But a real change happens through the center of your being, not through the circumference. Character is painting the circumference, consciousness is transformation of the center.

THE MOMENT YOU START SEEING YOUR FAULTS, THEY START DROPPING LIKE DRY LEAVES. Then nothing else has to be done. To see them is enough. Just to be aware of your faults is all that is needed. In that awareness they start disappearing, they evaporate.

One can go on committing a certain error only if one remains unconscious of it. Unconsciousness is a must to go on committing the same errors, and even if you try to change, you will commit the same error in some other form, in some other shape. They come in all sizes and all shapes! You will exchange, you will substitute, but you cannot drop it because deep down you don't see that it is a fault. Others may be telling you because they can see. . . .

That's why everybody thinks himself so beautiful, so intelligent, so virtuous, so saintly—and nobody agrees with him! The reason is simple: you look at others, you see their reality, and about yourself you carry fictions, beautiful fictions. All that you know about yourself is more or less a myth; it has nothing to do with reality.

The moment one sees one's faults, a radical change sets in. Hence all the buddhas down the ages have been teaching only one thing— awareness. They don't teach you character—character is taught by priests, politicians, but not by the bud-dhas. Buddhas teach you *consciousness* not *conscience*.

Conscience is a trick played upon you by others—others are telling you what is right and what is wrong. They are forcing their ideas upon you, and they go on forcing them from your very childhood. When you were so in-nocent, so vulnerable, so delicate that there was a possibility of making an im-pression on you, an imprint on you, they have conditioned you—from the very beginning. That conditioning is called conscience, and that conscience goes on dominating your whole life. Conscience is a strategy of society to enslave you.

The buddhas teach consciousness. Consciousness means you are not to learn from others what is right and what is wrong. There is no need to learn from anybody, you have simply to go in. Just the inward journey is enough—the deeper you go, the more consciousness is released. When you reach the center, you are so full of light that darkness disappears.

When you bring light into your room, you don't have to push the darkness out. The presence of the light is enough because darkness is only an absence of light. So are all your insanities, madnesses.

A man dressed as Adolf Hitler visited a psychiatrist.

"You can see I have no problems," he said. "I have the

> The moment one sees one's faults, a radical change sets in. Hence all the buddhas down the ages have been teaching only one thing—awareness. Character is taught by priests, politicians, but not by the buddhas. Buddhas teach you *consciousness*, not *conscience*.

greatest army in the world, all the money I will ever need, and every conceivable luxury you can imagine."

"Then what seems to be your problem?" asked the doctor.

"It's my wife," said the man. "She thinks she's Mrs. Weaver."

Don't laugh at the poor man. It is nobody else but you.

A man went into a tailor's shop and saw a man hanging by one arm from the center of the ceiling.

"What is he doing there?" the man asked the tailor.

"Oh, pay no attention," said the tailor, "he thinks he's a lightbulb."

"Well, why don't you tell him he's not?" asked the startled customer.

"What?" replied the tailor. "And work in the dark?"

The moment you know you are mad, you are no longer mad. That's the only criterion of sanity. The moment you know you are ignorant, you have become wise.

The oracle at Delphi declared Socrates the most wise man on the earth. A few people rushed to Socrates and told him, "Be pleased, rejoice! The oracle at Delphi has declared you the wisest man in the world."

Socrates said, "That is all nonsense. I know only one thing: that I know nothing."

The people were puzzled and confused. They went back to the temple, they told the oracle, "You say that Socrates is the wisest man in the world, but he himself denies it. On the contrary, he says he is utterly ignorant. He says he knows only one thing, that he knows nothing."

The oracle laughed and said, "That's why I have declared him the wisest man in the world. That's why—precisely because he knows that he is ignorant."

Ignorant people believe they are wise. Insane people believe they are the sanest.

And it is part of human nature that we go on looking to the outside. We watch everybody except ourselves; hence we know more about others than about ourselves. We know nothing about ourselves. We are not witnesses to our own functioning of the mind, we are not watchful inside.

You need a 180-degree turn—that's what meditation is all about. You have to close your eyes and start watching. In the beginning you will find only darkness and nothing else. And many people become frightened and rush out, because outside there is light.

> When you bring light into your room, you don't have to push the darkness out. The presence of the light is enough, because darkness is only an absence of light. So are all your insanities, madnesses.

Yes, there is light outside, but that light is not going to enlighten you, that light is not going to help you at all. You need inner light, a light that has its source in your very being, a light that cannot be extinguished even by death, a light that is eternal. And you have it, the potential is there! You are born with it, but you are keeping it behind you; you never look at it.

And because for centuries, for many lives, you have looked outside, it has become a mechanical habit. Even when you are asleep, you are looking at dreams—dreams mean reflections of the outside. When you close your eyes, you again start daydreaming or thinking; that means again you become interested in others. This has become such a chronic habit that there are not even small intervals, small windows, into your own being from where you can have a glimpse of who you are.

In the beginning it is a hard struggle, it is arduous. It is difficult—but not impossible. If you are decisive, if you are committed to inner exploration, then sooner or later it happens. You just have to go on digging, you have to go on struggling with the darkness. Soon you will pass the darkness and you will enter into the realm of light. And that light is true light, far truer than the light of the sun or the moon because all the lights that are outside are temporal; they are only for the time being. Even the sun is going to die one day. Not only do small lamps exhaust their resources and die in the morning, even the sun with such immense resources is dying every day. Sooner or later it will become a black hole; it will die and no light will come from it. Howsoever long it lives, it is not eternal. The inner light is eternal; it has no beginning, no end.

I am not interested in telling you to drop your faults, to make yourself good, to improve your character—no, not at all. I am not interested in your character at all; I am interested only in your consciousness.

Become more alert, more conscious. Just go deeper and deeper into yourself till you find the center of your being. You are living on the periphery, and on the periphery there is always turmoil. The deeper you go, the deeper the silence that prevails. And in those experiences of silence, light, joy, your life starts moving into a different dimension. The errors, the mistakes, start disappearing.

So don't be worried about the errors and the mistakes and the faults. Be concerned about one single thing, one single phenomenon. Put your total energy into one goal, and that is how to be more conscious, how to be more awakened. If you put your total energy into it, it is going to happen, it is inevitable. It is your birthright.

MORALITY IS CONCERNED WITH GOOD QUALITIES AND BAD QUALITIES. A man is good—according to morality—who is honest, truthful, authentic, trustworthy.

The man of awareness is not only a good man, he is much more. For the good man, goodness is all; for the man of awareness, goodness is just a by-product. The moment you are conscious of your own being, goodness follows you like a shadow. Then there is no need of any effort to be good; goodness becomes your nature. Just as the trees are green, you are good.

But the "good man" is not necessarily aware. His goodness is out of great effort, he is fighting with bad qualities—lying or stealing, untruthfulness, dishonesty, violence. They are in the good man but only repressed, they can erupt any moment.

> The good man can change into a bad man easily, without any effort—because all those bad qualities are there, only dormant, repressed with effort. If he removes the effort, they will immediately erupt in his life.

The good man can change into a bad man easily, without any effort—because all those bad qualities are there, only dormant, repressed with effort. If he removes the effort, they will immediately erupt in his life. And the good qualities are only cultivated, not natural. He has tried hard to be honest, to be sincere, not to lie—but it has been an effort, it has been tiring.

The good man is always serious, because he is afraid of all the bad qualities he has repressed. And he is serious because deep down he desires to be honored for his goodness, to be rewarded. His longing is to be respectable. Your so-called saints are mostly just "good men."

There is only one way to transcend the "good man," and that is by bringing more awareness to your being. Awareness is not something to be cultivated; it is already there, it has just to be awakened. When you are totally awakened, whatever you do is good, and whatever you do not do is bad.

The good man has to make immense efforts to do good and to avoid the bad; the bad is a constant temptation for him. It is a choice: every moment he has to choose the good, and not to choose the bad. For example, a man like Mahatma Gandhi—he is a good man; he tried hard his whole life to be on the side of good. But even at the age of seventy he was having sexual dreams, and he was very much in anguish: "As far as my waking hours are concerned, I can keep myself completely free from sex. But what can I do in sleep? All that I repress in the day comes in the night."

It shows one thing, that it has not gone anywhere; it has been inside you, just waiting. The moment you relax, the moment you remove the effort—and asleep you have at least to relax and remove the effort to be good—all the bad qualities that you have been repressing will start becoming your dreams. Your dreams are your repressed desires.

The good man is in continuous conflict. His life is not one of joy; he cannot laugh wholeheartedly, he cannot sing, he cannot dance. In everything he continually makes judgments. His mind is full of condemnation and judgment—and because he is himself trying hard to be good, he is judging others also by the same criteria. He cannot accept you as you are; he can accept you only if you fulfill his demands of being good. And because he cannot accept people as they are, he condemns them. All your saints are full of condemnation of everybody; according to them you are all sinners.

These are not the qualities of the authentic religious man. The authentically religious man has no judgment, no condemnation. He knows one thing, that no act is good and no act is bad—awareness is good and unawareness is bad. You may even do something, in unawareness, that looks good to the whole world, but to the religious man it is not good. And you may do something bad, and you will be condemned by everybody *except* by the religious man. He cannot condemn you—because you are unconscious; you need compassion, not judgment. Not condemnation—you don't deserve hell, nobody deserves hell.

Coming to a point of absolute awareness, there is no question of choice—you simply do whatever is good. You do it innocently, just as your shadow follows you, with no effort. If you run, the shadow runs; if you stop, the shadow stops—but there is no effort on the part of the shadow.

> ⤜⤛
>
> Coming to a point of absolute awareness, there is no question of choice—you simply do whatever is good. You do it innocently, just as your shadow follows you, with no effort.

The man of awareness cannot be thought synonymous with the good man. He *is* good—but in such a different way, from such a different angle. He is good not because he is *trying* to be good; he is good because he is aware. And in awareness, bad, evil, all those condemnatory words, disappear as darkness disappears in light.

Religions have decided to remain only moralities. They are ethical codes; they are useful for society, but not useful for you, not useful for the individual. They are conveniences created by society. Naturally, if everybody starts stealing, life will become impossible; if everybody starts lying, life will be become impossible; if everybody is dishonest, you cannot exist at all. So on the lowest level, morality is needed by society; it is a social utility, but it is not a religious revolution.

Don't be satisfied by just being good.

Remember, you have to come to a point where you need not even think about what is good and what is bad. Your very awareness, your very consciousness, simply takes you toward that which is good—there is no repression. I would not call Mahatma Gandhi a man of awareness, only a good man—and he tried really hard to be good. I do not suspect his intentions, but he was obsessed with goodness.

A man of awareness is not obsessed with anything—he has no obsession. He is just relaxed, calm and quiet, silent and serene. Out of his silence whatever blossoms is good. It is always good—he lives in a choiceless awareness.

So go beyond the ordinary concept of a good man. You will not be good, you will not be bad. You will be simply alert, conscious, aware, and then whatever follows is going to be good. In a different way I can say that in your total awareness you attain the quality of godliness—and good is only a small by-product of godliness.

Religions have been teaching you to be good, so that one day you can find God. That is not possible—no good man has ever found godliness. I am teaching just the reverse: find godliness, and good will come on its own accord. And when good comes on its own accord, it has a beauty, a grace, a simplicity, a humbleness. It does not ask for any reward here or hereafter. It is its own reward.

EXPERIMENTS IN WATCHING

People are watching only others; they never bother to watch themselves. Everybody is watching—that is the most superficial watching—what the other person is doing, what the other person is
wearing, how he looks. . . . Everybody is watching; watching is not
something new to be introduced in your life. It has only to be
deepened, taken away from others, and arrowed toward your own
inner feelings, thoughts, moods—and finally, the watcher itself.

A Jew is sitting in a train opposite a priest. "Tell me,
Your Worship," the Jew asks, "why do you wear your
collar back to front?"

"Because I am a father," answers the priest.

"I am also a father, and I don't wear my collar like
that."

"Oh," says the priest, "but I am a father to
thousands."

"Then maybe," replies the Jew, "it is your trousers
you should wear back to front."

People are very watchful about everybody else.

Two guys went out for a walk; suddenly it began to rain.
"Quick," said one man, "open your umbrella."

"It won't help," said his friend, "my umbrella is full
of holes."

"Then why did you bring it in the first place?"
"I did not think it would rain."

You can laugh easily about the ridiculous acts of other people, but have you ever laughed about yourself? Have you ever caught yourself doing something ridiculous? No, you keep yourself completely unwatched. Your whole watching is about others, and that is not of any help.

TIME YOURSELF INTO TIMELESSNESS

If you just put a watch with a second hand in front of you and keep your eyes on the second hand, you will be surprised—you cannot continue to remember even for one minute completely. Perhaps fifteen seconds, twenty seconds, at the most thirty seconds, and you will forget. You will get lost in some other idea—and then suddenly you will remember that you were trying to remember. Even to keep awareness continuous for one minute is difficult, so one has to be aware that it is not child's play. When you are trying to be aware of the small things of life, you have to remember that many times you will forget. You will go far away into something else. The moment you remember, don't feel guilty—that is one of the traps.

If you start feeling guilty, then you cannot come back to the awareness that you were practicing. There is no need to feel guilty, it is natural. Don't feel repentance—it is natural, and it happens to every seeker. Accept it as natural; otherwise you will be caught in repentance, in feeling guilty that you cannot remember even for a few moments and you go on forgetting.

The Jain master Mahavira is the first man in history who has actually worked out that if a man can remember, can be aware, for forty-eight minutes continuously, that's enough—he will become enlightened, nobody can prevent him. Just forty-eight minutes—but it is difficult even for forty-eight seconds! So many distractions . . .

No guilt, no repentance—the moment you remember that you have forgotten what you were doing, simply come back. Simply come back and start working again. Don't cry and weep for the spilled milk, that is stupid.

It will take time, but slowly you will become aware that you are remaining alert more and more, perhaps for a whole minute, perhaps two minutes. And it is such a joy that you have been aware for two minutes—but don't get caught in the joy, don't think that you have attained something. That will become a barrier. These are patterns where one is lost—just a little gain and one thinks one has come home.

Go on working slowly, patiently. There is no hurry—you have eternity at your disposal. Don't try to be speedy. That impatience will not help. Awareness is not like seasonal flowers that grow in six weeks' time and are then gone. Awareness is like the cedars of Lebanon, which take hundreds of years to grow but they remain for thousands of years and rise to one hundred and fifty feet, two hundred feet high in the sky.

Awareness grows slowly, but it grows. One just has to be patient.

As it grows, you will start feeling many things that you have never felt before. For example, you will start feeling that you are carrying many tensions in your body of which you have never been aware because they are subtle tensions. Now your awareness is there, you can feel those subtle, delicate tensions. So wherever you feel any tension in the body, relax that part. If your whole body is relaxed, your awareness will grow faster because those tensions are hindrances.

As your awareness grows even more, you will be surprised to know that you don't dream only in sleep; there is an undercurrent of dreaming even while you are awake. It goes just underneath your wakefulness—close your eyes any moment and you can see some dream passing by like a cloud in the sky. But only when you become a little more aware will it be possible to see that your wakefulness is not true awakening. The dream is floating there—people call it a daydream. If they relax in their chair for a moment and close their eyes, immediately the dream takes over. They start thinking that they have become the president of the country, or they are doing great things—or anything, which they know at the very moment they are dreaming is all nonsense. You are not the president of the country, but still the dream has something in it such that it continues in spite of you. Awareness will make you aware of layers of dreams in your waking state. And they will start dispersing, just as you bring light into a dark room and the darkness starts dispersing.

THE INVISIBLE TOUCH

Whatsoever you are doing—walking, sitting, eating, or if you are not doing anything, just breathing, resting, relaxing in the grass—never forget that you are a watcher.

You will forget it again and again. You will get involved in some thought, some feeling, some emotion, some sentiment—anything will distract you from the watcher. Remember, and run back to your center of watching.

Make it an inner process, continuously. . . . You will be surprised at how life changes its whole quality. I can move my hand without any watchfulness, and I can also move my hand absolutely watching from inside the whole movement. The movements are totally different. The first movement is a robot movement, mechanical. The second movement is a conscious movement. And when you are conscious, you feel that hand from within; when you are not conscious, you only know the hand from without.

You have known your face only in the mirror, from the without, because you are not a watcher. If you start watching, you will feel your face from within—and that is such an experience, to watch yourself from within. Then slowly, strange things start happening. Thoughts disappear, feelings disappear, emotions disappear, and there is a silence surrounding you. You are just like an island in the middle of the ocean of silence . . . just a watcher, as if a flame of light is at the center of your being, radiating the whole of your being.

In the beginning it will only be an inner experience. Slowly you will see that radiation spreading out of your body, those rays reaching other people. You will be surprised and shocked that other people, if they are a little bit sensitive, will immediately become aware that something has touched them, which was not visible. For example, if you are watching yourself, just walk behind somebody, watching yourself, and it is almost certain the person will turn and look back suddenly, for no reason. When you are watching yourself, your watchfulness starts radiating, and it is bound to touch the person who is ahead of you. And if he is touched by something that is invisible, he is going to look back: "What is the matter?" And you are so away you cannot even touch him with your hand.

You can try an experiment: somebody is sleeping and you can sit by their side, just watching yourself, and the person will suddenly wake up, open his eyes, and look all around as if somebody has touched him.

Slowly you will also become able to feel the touch through the rays. That is what is called the vibe. It is not a nonexistential thing. The other person feels it; you will also feel that you have touched the other person.

The English term, being touched, is used very significantly. You may use it without understanding what it means when you say "I was touched" by the person. He may not have said a single word to you. He may just have passed by. He may just have looked once at your eyes, and you feel "touched" by the person. It is not just a word—it actually happens. And then those rays go on spreading to people, to animals, to trees, to rocks . . . and one day you will see, you are touching the whole universe from within.

VIPASSANA

Buddha's way was *vipassana*—*vipassana* means witnessing. And he found one of the greatest devices ever, the device of watching your breath—just watching your breath. Breathing is such a simple and natural phenomenon, and it is there twenty-four hours a day. You need not make any effort. If you repeat a mantra, then you will have to make an effort, you will have to force yourself. If you say, "Ram, Ram, Ram," you will have to continuously strain yourself. And you are bound to forget many times. Moreover, the word *Ram* is again something of the mind, and anything of the mind can never lead you beyond the mind.

Buddha discovered a totally different angle. Just watch your breath—the breath coming in, the breath going out.

There are four points to be watched. Sitting silently, just start seeing the breath, feeling the breath. The breath going in is the first point. Then for a moment when the breath is in, it stops—a small moment it is, for a split second it stops; that is the second point to watch. Then the breath turns and goes out; this is the third point to watch. Then again, when the breath is completely out, for a split second it stops. That is the fourth point to watch. Then the breath starts coming in again . . . this is the circle of breath. If you can watch all these four points, you will be surprised, amazed, at the miracle of such a simple process—because mind is not involved.

Watching is not a quality of the mind; watching is the quality of the soul, of consciousness. Watching is not a mental process at all. When you watch, the mind stops, ceases to be. Yes, in the beginning many times you will forget and the mind will come in and start playing its old games. But whenever you remember that you have forgotten, there is no need to feel repentant, guilty—just go back to watching, again and again go back to watching your breath. Slowly, slowly, less and less the mind interferes.

And when you can watch your breath for forty-eight minutes as a continuum, you will become enlightened. You will be surprised—just forty-eight minutes? Because you will think that it is not very difficult . . . just forty-eight minutes! It is very difficult. Forty-eight seconds and you will have fallen victim to the mind many times! Try it with a watch in front of you; in the beginning you cannot be watchful for sixty seconds. In just sixty seconds, that is one minute, you will fall asleep many times. You will forget all about watching—the watch and the watching will both be forgotten. Some idea will take you far, far away; then suddenly you will realize . . . you will look at the watch and ten seconds have passed. For ten seconds you were not watching.

But slowly, slowly—it is a knack; it is not a practice, it is a knack—slowly, slowly you imbibe it. Because those few moments when you are watchful are of such exquisite beauty, of such tremendous joy, that once you have tasted those few moments, you would like to come back again and again—not for any other motive, just for the sheer joy of being there, present to the breath.

Remember, it is not the same process as is done in Yoga. In Yoga the process is called *pranayam;* it is a totally different process, in fact just the opposite of what Buddha calls *vipassana.* In *pranayam* you take deep breaths, you fill your chest with more and more air, more and more oxygen; then you empty your chest as totally as possible of all carbon dioxide. It is a physical exercise—good for the body, but it has nothing to do with *vipassana.*

In *vipassana* you are not to change the rhythm of your natural breath. You are not to take long, deep breaths, you are not to exhale in any way differently than you ordinarily do. Let it be absolutely normal and natural. Your whole consciousness has to be on one point, watching.

And if you can watch your breath, then you can start watching other things too. Walking you can watch that you are walking, eating you can watch that you are eating. And ultimately, finally, you can watch that you are sleeping. The day you can watch that you are sleeping, you are transported into another world. The body goes on sleeping, and inside a light goes on burning brightly. Your watchfulness remains undisturbed. Then twenty-four hours a day there is an undercurrent of watching. You go on doing things . . . for the outside world nothing has changed, but for you everything has changed.

A Zen master was carrying water from a well, and a devotee who had heard about him and had traveled far to see him asked, "Where can I see so-and-so, the master of this monastery?" He thought this man must be a servant, carrying water from the well—you cannot find a buddha carrying water from a well, you cannot find a buddha cleaning the floor.

The master laughed and said, "I am the person you are seeking."

The devotee could not believe it. "I have heard much about you, but I cannot conceive of you carrying water from the well."

The master said, "But that's what I used to do before I became enlightened. Carrying water from the well, chopping wood—that's what I used to do before, and that's what I continue to do. I am very proficient in these two things: carrying water from the well and chopping wood. Come with me—my next thing is going to be chopping wood, watch me!"

"But then what is the difference? Before enlightenment you used to do these two things, after enlightenment you are doing the same two things—then what is the difference?"

The master laughed. "The difference is inner. Before, I was doing everything in sleep; now I am doing everything consciously, that's the difference. Activities are the same, but I am no longer the same. The world is the same, but I am not the same. And because I am no longer the same, for me the world is also no longer the same."

The transformation has to be inner. This is real renunciation: the old world is gone because the old being is gone.

THE NIGHT SHIFT

The phenomena of dreaming and watchfulness are totally different things. Just try one thing: every night, going to sleep, while you are just half-awake, half-asleep, slowly going deeper into sleep, repeat to yourself, "I will be able to remember that it is a dream."

Go on repeating it till you fall asleep. It will take a few days, but one day you will be surprised: once this idea sinks deep into the unconscious, you can watch the dream as a dream. Then it has no grip over you. Then slowly, as your watchfulness becomes more sharp, dreams will disappear. They are very shy; they don't want to be watched. They exist only in the darkness of the unconscious. As watchfulness brings light in, they start disappearing.

So go on doing the same exercise, and you can get rid of dreams. And you will be surprised: getting rid of dreams has many implications. If the dreams disappear, then in the daytime your mind's chattering will not be so much as it used to be. Secondly, you will be more in the moment—not in the future, not in the past. Thirdly, your intensity, your totality of action, will increase.

Dreaming is a disease. It is needed because man is sick. But if dreams can be completely dropped, you will attain a new kind of health, a new vision. And part of your unconscious mind will become conscious, so you will have a stronger individuality. Whatever you do, you will never repent, because you will have done it with such consciousness that repentance has no relevance.

Watchfulness is the greatest magic that one can learn, because it can begin the transformation of your whole being.

WHEN YOU START WATCHING YOUR DREAMS, YOU WILL FIND FIVE TYPES OF DREAMS HAPPENING. The first type of dream is just rubbish—and many thousands of psychoanalysts are just working on that rubbish. It is simply useless. It happens because in the whole day, working the whole day, you gather much rubbish. Just as the body gathers dust and you need a bath, you need a cleaning, in the same way the mind gathers dust. And there is no way to give a bath to the mind, so the mind has an automatic mechanism to throw out all dust and rubbish. The dream is nothing but the raising of the dust that the mind is throwing—the first type of dream—and this is the biggest portion of dreams, almost 90 percent. Almost 90 percent of dreams are simply dust being thrown. Don't pay much attention to them. And by and by, as your awareness grows, you will be able to see what is dust.

The second type of dream is a sort of wish fulfillment. There are many needs, natural needs, but the priests and the so-called religious teachers have poisoned your mind. They won't allow you even to fulfill your basic needs. They have condemned them completely, and the condemnation has entered you. So you hunger for many of your needs—those hungry needs demand fulfillment, and the second type of dreaming is nothing but wish fulfillment. Whatsoever you have denied to your being because of the priests and the poisoners, the mind tries to fulfill it in dreams, in some way or other.

But one should look to the need, not to the meaning. Meaning is of the conscious mind, need is of the unconscious—and that's how the second type of dream comes into existence. You go on cutting your needs, then the mind fulfills them in dream. You have read great books, and you are poisoned by thinkers, and they have molded your mind in certain patterns. You are no longer open to existence itself; philosophies have blinded you—then you will start cutting your needs. Then those needs will bubble up, surface in the dream, because the unconscious knows no philosophies. The unconscious knows no meaning, no purpose. The unconscious knows only one thing: what is needed for your being to become fulfilled. Then the unconscious forces its own dreaming. This is the second type of dream; very meaningful to understand it and meditate on it. Because the unconscious is trying to communicate to you, "Don't be a fool! You will suffer for it. And don't starve your being. Don't be suicidal, and don't go on committing a slow suicide by killing your needs."

Remember: desires are of the conscious mind, needs of the unconscious. And the distinction is very, very meaningful, very significant to be understood.

Desires are of the conscious mind—the unconscious knows no desires, the unconscious is not worried about desires. What is a desire? A desire comes out of your thinking, training, conditioning. You would like to be the president of the country—the unconscious does not bother about it. The unconscious is not interested in being the president of the country, the unconscious is interested only in how to be a fulfilled, organic unity. But the conscious mind says, "Become a president, and if in becoming the president you have to sacrifice your love, then sacrifice. If you have to sacrifice your body—sacrifice. If you have to sacrifice rest—sacrifice. First become the president of the country." Or gathering too much wealth—that is of the conscious mind. The unconscious knows no wealth, the unconscious knows only the natural. It is untouched by the society; it is like animals or the birds, or like the trees. The unconscious has not been conditioned by the society, by the politicians. It remains yet pure.

Listen to the second type of the dream and meditate on it, and it will communicate to you what is your need. Fulfill the needs and don't bother about the desires. If you really want to be blissful, fulfill the needs and don't bother about desires. If you want to be miserable, cut the needs and follow the desires.

That's how you have become miserable. It is a simple phenomenon, whether you are miserable or blissful—very simple is the phenomenon. A man who listens to his needs and follows them, just like a river flows to the ocean. The river doesn't say whether to flow to the east or to the west, it simply seeks the way. East or west makes no difference. The river flowing to the ocean knows no desires; it knows only its needs. That's why animals look so happy—having nothing, and so happy? And you having so many things and so miserable? Even animals surpass you in their beauty, in their bliss. What is happening? The animals don't have a conscious mind to control and manipulate the unconscious; they remain undivided.

The second type of dream has much to reveal to you. With the second type you start changing your consciousness, you start changing your behavior, you start changing your life pattern. Listen to your needs, whatsoever the unconscious is saying.

Always remember: the unconscious is right, because it has the wisdom of the ages. Millions of lives you have existed; the conscious belongs to this life. It has been trained in the schools and the universities, and by the family and the society in which you were born—coincidentally born. But the unconscious carries all the experiences of all your lives. It carries the experience of when you were a rock, it carries the experience of when you were a tree, it carries the experience of when you were animals—it carries all, the whole past. The unconscious is tremendously wise, and the conscious is tremendously foolish—has to be so, because the conscious is just of this life, very small, with no experience. It is childish. The unconscious is eternal wisdom. Listen to it.

Now the whole of psychoanalysis in the West is doing only this and nothing else: listening to the second type of dreaming and changing your life pattern accordingly. And psychoanalysis has helped many people. It has its own limitations, but it has helped because at least this part, listening to the second type of dreaming, makes your life more relaxed, less tense.

Then there is a third type of dream. This third type of dream is a communication from the superconscious. The second type of dream is a communication from the unconscious. The third type of dream is rare, because we have lost all contact with the superconscious. But still it comes, because the superconscious is yours. Maybe it has become a cloud and moved into the sky, evaporated, maybe the distance is very far, but it is anchored still in you.

The communication from the superconscious is rare. When you become very, very alert, only then you will start feeling it. Otherwise, it will be lost in the dust that the mind throws in dreams, and the wish fulfillment that the mind goes on dreaming about—things incomplete, suppressed. It will be lost. But when you become aware, it is just like a diamond shining—absolutely different from all the stones around.

When you can feel and find a dream that is coming from the superconscious, watch it. Meditate on it, because that will become your guidance, that will lead to your master. That will lead you to the way of life that can suit you, that will lead you to the right discipline. That dream will become a deep guide inside. With the conscious you can find a master, but the master will be nothing more than a teacher. With the unconscious you can find a master, but the master will not be more than a lover—you will fall in love with a certain personality, with a certain type. But only the superconscious can lead you to the right master. Then he is not a teacher; you are not infatuated with what he says, you are not infatuated with what he is. Rather, on the contrary, you are guided by your superconscious that this man will suit you, that this man will provide the right possibility for you to grow, that this man can become your soil.

Then there is a fourth type of dream, which comes from past lives. Not rare—many times it comes. But everything is a mess inside you; you cannot make any distinctions. You are not there to make distinctions.

In the East we have worked hard on this fourth type of dream. Because of this type of dream we stumbled upon the phenomenon of reincarnation. From this type of dream you become, by and by, aware of your past lives—you move backward, backward in time. Then many things start changing in you—because if you can remember, even in a dream, who you were in your past life, many things will become meaningless and many new things will become meaningful. The whole pattern will change, your gestalt will change.

Because you accumulated too much wealth in a past life, you died the richest man in the country and deep down a beggar—and again you are doing the same in this life. Suddenly the gestalt will change. If you can remember what you did and how it all came to nothing—if you can remember many lives, many times you have been doing the same again and again; you are like a stuck gramophone record, a vicious circle, again you start the same and you end the same—if you can remember a few of your lives, you will suddenly be surprised that you have never done a single thing new. Again and again you accumulated wealth; again and again you tried to be powerful politically; again and again you became too knowledgeable. Again and again you fell in love, and again and again the same misery that love brings . . . when you see this repetition, how can you remain the same? Then this life is suddenly transfigured. You cannot remain in the same rut anymore.

That's why in the East, people have been asking for millennia, "How to get out of this wheel of life and death?" It seems to be the same wheel, it seems to be the same story again and again—a repetition. If you don't know it, then you think you are doing new things, and you are so excited. And I can see you have been doing these same things again and again.

Nothing is new in life; it is a wheel. It moves on the same route. Because you go on forgetting about the past, that's why you feel so much excitement. Once you remember, the whole excitement drops. In that remembrance happens *sannyas*.

Sannyas is an effort to get out of the rut, it is an effort to jump out of the wheel. It is to say to yourself, "Enough is enough! Now I am not going to participate anymore in the same old nonsense. I am getting out of it." *Sannyas* is a perfect dropping out of the wheel—not out of the society, but out of your own inner wheel of life and death.

This is the fourth type of dream.

And then there is a fifth type of dream, and the last type—the fourth type is going backward into your past, the fifth type is going forward into the future. Rare, very rare—it happens only sometimes; when you are very, very vulnerable, open, flexible. The past gives a shadow and the future gives a shadow, it reflects in you. If you can become aware of your dreams, someday you will become aware of this possibility also—that the future looks into you. Just suddenly a door opens and the future has a communication with you.

These are the five types of dreams. Modern psychology understands only the second type and often confuses it with the first type. The other three types are almost unknown.

If you meditate and become aware of your inner being in dreams, many more things will happen. The first—by and by, the more you become aware of your dreams, the less and less will you be convinced of the reality of your waking hours. Hence, Hindus say that the world is like a dream.

Right now just the opposite is the case. Because you are so convinced of the reality of the world in your waking hours, you think while you dream that those dreams are also real. Nobody feels while dreaming that the dream is unreal—while dreaming, it looks perfect, it looks absolutely real. In the morning of course you may say it was just a dream—but that is not the point, because now another mind is functioning. *This* mind was not a witness at all; *this* mind has only heard the rumor. This conscious mind that wakes in the morning and says it was all dream—this mind was not a witness at all, so how can this mind say anything? He has simply heard a rumor.

It is as if you are asleep and two persons are talking, and you—in your sleep, because they are talking so loudly—just hear some words from here and there, and just a hodgepodge impression is left. This is happening—while the unconscious creates dreams, and tremendous activity goes on, the conscious is asleep and just hears the rumor and in the morning says, "It is all false. It was just a dream."

Right now, whenever you dream, you feel it is absolutely real. Even absurd things look real, illogical things look real, because the unconscious knows no logic. You are walking on a road in a dream, you see a horse coming, and suddenly the horse is no longer a horse, the horse has become your wife. And nothing happens to your mind, to question "How can it be possible? The horse has so suddenly become my wife?" No problem arises, no doubt arises. The unconscious knows no doubt. Even such an absurd phenomenon is believed; you are convinced of the reality.

Just the opposite happens when you become aware of the dreams and you feel they are really dreams—nothing is real, just mind drama, a psychodrama. You are the stage, and you are the actors, and you are the storywriter. You are the director, and you are the producer, and you are the spectator—nobody else there, it is just a mind creation. When you become aware of this, then this whole world that exists while you are awake will change its quality. Then you will see that here also, the same is the case—on a wider stage, but the dream is the same.

Hindus also call this world *maya*—illusory, dreamlike, mind-stuff. What do they mean? Do they mean that it is unreal? No, it is not unreal—but when your mind gets mixed into it, you create an unreal world of your own. We don't live in the same world; everybody lives in his own world. There are as many worlds as there are minds. When Hindus say that these worlds are *maya,* they mean the reality plus mind is *maya.* Reality, that which is, we don't know. Reality plus mind is illusion, *maya.*

When somebody becomes totally awakened, a buddha, then he knows reality *minus* mind. Then it is the truth, the *brahman,* the ultimate. Plus mind, and everything becomes dream, because mind is the stuff that creates dreams. Minus mind, nothing can be a dream; only reality remains, in its crystal purity.

Mind is just like a mirror. In the mirror, the world is reflected. That reflection cannot be real, that reflection is just a reflection. When the mirror is no longer there, the reflection disappears—now you can see the real. A full-moon night, and the lake is silent and the moon is reflected in the lake and you try to catch the moon. This is all that everybody has been doing for many lives—trying to catch the moon in the mirror of the lake. And of course you never succeed—you cannot succeed, it is not possible. One has to forget about the lake and look exactly in the opposite direction. There is the moon. Mind is the lake in which the world becomes illusory. Whether you dream with closed eyes or you dream with open eyes makes no difference—if the mind is there, all that happens is dream.

This will be the first realization if you meditate on dreams.

And the second realization will be that you are a witness: the dream is there but you are not part of it. You are not part of your mind, you are a transcendence. You are in the mind but you are not the mind. You look through the mind but you are not the mind. You use the mind but you are not the mind. Suddenly you are a witness—no longer a mind.

And this witnessing is the final, the ultimate, realization. Then, whether the dream happens while asleep or the dream happens while awake makes no difference—you remain a witness. You remain in the world, but the world cannot enter in you anymore. Things are there but the mind is not in the things, and the things are not in the mind. Suddenly the witness comes in and everything changes.

It is simple once you know the knack of it. Otherwise, it looks difficult, almost impossible—how to be awake while dreaming? It looks impossible but it is not. Three to nine months it will take, if every night when you go to sleep, while falling into sleep, you are trying to be alert and watching it.

But remember, don't try to be alert in an *active* sense; otherwise you will not be able to fall asleep. Passive alertness—loose, natural, relaxed, just looking out of the corner of your eye. Not too active about it—just passive awareness, not too concerned. Sitting by the side, and the river flows by and you are just watching. Three to nine months this takes. Then someday, suddenly the sleep is falling on you like a dark screen, like a dark curtain—as if the sun has set and the night is descending. It settles all around you, but deep inside a flame goes on burning. You are watching—silent, passive. Then the world of dream starts. Then many plays happen, many psychodramas, and you go on watching. By and by, the distinction comes into existence—now you can see what type of dream it is. Then suddenly, one day you realize that this is the same as while waking. There is no difference of quality. The whole world has become illusory. And when the world is illusory, only the witness is real.

Afterword

HANGING BY A THREAD

There is an ancient story in India:

A great sage sent his chief disciple to the court of King Janak to learn something that was missing in the young man.

The young man said, "If you can't teach me, how can this man Janak teach it to me? You are a great sage, he is only a king. What does he know about meditation and awareness?"

The great sage said, "You simply follow my instructions. Go to him, bow down to him; don't be egoistic, thinking that you are a *sannyasi* and he is only an ordinary house-holder, that he lives in the world, he is worldly and you are spiritual. Forget all about that. I'm sending you to him to learn something, so for this moment, he is your master. And I know, I have tried here, but you cannot understand because you need a different context to understand it. The court of Janak and his palace will give you the right context. You simply go, bow down to him. For these few days, he will represent me."

Reluctantly, the young man went. He was a Brahmin, of high caste! And what was this Janak? He was rich, he had a great kingdom, but what could he teach a Brahmin? Brahmins always think that they can teach people. And Janak was not a Brahmin, he was a Kshatriya, the warrior caste in India. They are thought to be second to Brahmins; the Brahmins are the first, the foremost, the highest caste. To bow down to this man? This has never been done! A Brahmin bowing down to a Kshatriya is against the Indian mind.

But the master had said it, so it had to be done. Reluctantly the young man went, and reluctantly he bowed down. And when he bowed down, he was really feeling angry with his master because having to bow down to Janak was so ugly in his eyes. A beautiful woman was dancing in the court, and people were drinking wine, and Janak was sitting in this group. The young man had such condemnation—but still, he bowed down.

Janak laughed and said, "You need not bow down to me when you are carrying such condemnation in you. And don't be so prejudiced before you have experienced me. Your master knows me well, that's why he has sent you here. He has sent you to learn something, but this is not the way to learn."

The young man said, "I don't care. He has sent me, I have come, but by the morning I will go back because I can't see that I can learn anything here. In fact, if I learn anything from you, my whole life will be wasted! I have not come to learn drinking wine and seeing a beautiful woman dance, and all this indulgence."

Janak still smiled and said, "You can go in the morning. But since you have come and you are so tired . . . at least rest for the night and in the morning you can go. And who knows—the night may become the context of the learning for which your master has sent you to me."

Now, this was mysterious. How could the night teach him anything? But okay, he had to be here for the night, so don't make much fuss about it. He remained. The king arranged for him to have the most beautiful room in the palace, the most luxurious. The king went with the young man, took every care about his food, his sleep, and when he had gone to bed, Janak left.

But the young man could not sleep the whole night, because as he looked up, he could see a naked sword hanging by a thin thread just above his head. Now, it was so dangerous that at any moment the sword could fall and kill the young man. So he remained awake the whole night, watchful, so he could avoid the catastrophe if it was going to happen. In the morning the king asked, "Was the bed comfortable, the room comfortable?"

The young man said, "Comfortable! Everything was comfortable—but what about the sword? Why did you play such a trick? It was so cruel! I was tired, I had come on foot from the faraway ashram of my master in the forest, and you played such a cruel joke. What kind of thing is this, to hang a naked sword by so thin a thread that I was afraid that just a small breeze and I am gone, finished. I have not come here to commit suicide."

The king said, "I want to ask only one thing. You were so tired, you could have fallen asleep easily, but you could not fall asleep. What happened? The danger was great, it was a question of life and death. Hence you were aware, alert. This is my teaching too. You can go. Or if you want, you can stay a few more days to watch me.

"Although I was sitting there in the court, where a beautiful woman was dancing, I was alert to the naked sword above my head. It is invisible; its name is death. I was not looking at the young woman. Just as you could not enjoy the luxury of the room, I was not drinking wine. I was just aware of death, which could come any moment. I am constantly aware of death; hence I live in the palace and yet I am a hermit. Your master knows me and understands me. He understands my understanding too. That's why he has sent you here. If you live here for a few days, you can watch on your own."

You want to know how to become more aware? Become more aware of the precariousness of life. Death can happen any moment—the next moment it may knock on your door. You can remain unaware if you think you are going to live forever—how can you live unaware if death is always close by? Impossible! If life is momentary, a soap bubble, just a pinprick and it is gone forever . . . how can you remain unaware?

Bring awareness to each act.

THERE ARE TWO PLANES IN YOU: THE PLANE OF THE MIND, AND THE PLANE OF THE NO-MIND. Or, let me say it in this way: the plane when you are on the periphery of your being and the plane when you are at the center of your being.

Every circle has a center—you may know it, you may not know it. You may not even suspect that there is a center, but there has to be. You are a periphery, you are a circle—there is a center. Without the center you cannot be; there is a nucleus of your being.

At that center you are already a buddha, one who has already arrived home. On the periphery, you are in the world—in the mind, in dreams, in desires, in anxieties, in a thousand and one games. And you are both.

There are bound to be moments when you will see that you have been for a few moments like a buddha—the same grace, the same awareness, the same silence; the same world of beati-

> You want to know how to become more aware? Become more aware of the precariousness of life. Death can happen any moment—the next moment it may knock on your door.

> ❧
>
> At the center you are already a buddha, one who has already arrived home. On the periphery, you are in the world—in the mind, in dreams, in desires, in anxieties, in a thousand and one games. And you are both.

tudes, of blessings, of benediction. There will be moments, glimpses of your own center—they cannot be permanent; again and again you will be thrown back to the periphery. And you will feel stupid, sad, frustrated; missing the meaning of life—because you exist on two planes, the plane of the periphery and the plane of the center.

But by and by, you will become capable of moving from the periphery to the center and from the center to the periphery very smoothly—just as you walk into your house and out of your house. You don't create any dichotomy. You don't say, "I am outside the house so how can I go inside the house?" You don't say, "I am inside the house so how can I come outside the house?" It is sunny outside, it is warm, pleasant— you sit outside in the garden. Then it is becoming hotter and hotter, and you start perspiring. Now it is no longer pleasant, it is becoming uncomfortable—you simply get up and move inside the house. There it is cool; there it is not uncomfortable. Now, it is inside the house that is pleasant. You go on moving in and out.

In the same way, a man of awareness and understanding moves from the periphery to the center, from the center to the periphery. He never gets fixated anywhere. From the marketplace to the monastery, from being extrovert to being introvert—he continuously goes on moving because these two are his wings. They are not against each other. They may be balanced in opposite directions—they have to be; if both the wings are on one side, the bird cannot fly into the sky. They have to be balancing, they have to be in opposite directions, but still they belong to the same bird, and they serve the same bird. Your outside and your inside are your wings.

> A man of awareness and understanding moves from the periphery to the center, from the center to the periphery. From the marketplace to the monastery, from being extrovert to being introvert—he continuously goes on moving because these two are his wings. They are not against each other.

This has to be very deeply remembered, because there is a possibility . . . the mind tends to fixate. There are people who are fixated in the marketplace; they say they cannot get out of it; they say they have no time for meditation; they say even if time is there, they don't know how to meditate and they don't believe that they can meditate. They say they are worldly—how can they meditate? They are materialistic—how can they meditate? They say, "Unfortunately, we are extroverts—how can we go in?" They have chosen only one wing. And of course, if frustration comes out of it, it is natural. With one wing frustration is bound to come.

Then there are people who become fed up with the world and escape out of the world, go to the monasteries and the Himalayas, become *sannyasins*, monks, start living alone, force a life of introversion on themselves. They close their eyes, they close all their doors and windows, they become like Leibniz's monads—windowless—then they are bored.

In the marketplace they were fed up, they were tired, frustrated. It was getting more like a madhouse; they could not find rest. There was too much of relationship and not enough holiday, not enough space to be themselves. They were falling into things, losing their beings; they were becoming more and more material and less and less spiritual. They were losing their direction. They were losing the very consciousness that they are. They escaped. Fed up, frustrated, they escaped. Now they are trying to live alone, a life of introversion—sooner or later they get bored. Again they have chosen another wing, but again only one wing. This is the way of a lopsided life. They have again fallen into the same fallacy on the opposite pole.

I am neither for this nor for that. I would like you to become so capable that you can remain in the marketplace and yet meditative. I would like you to relate with people, to love, to move in millions of relationships, because they enrich you—and yet remain capable of closing your doors and sometimes having a holiday from all relationship . . . so that you can relate with your own being also.

Relate with others, but relate with yourself also. Love others, but love yourself also. Go out!—the world is beautiful, adventurous; it is a challenge, it enriches. Don't lose that opportunity—whenever the world knocks at your door and calls you, go out. Go out fearlessly—there is nothing to lose, there is everything to gain. But don't get lost. Don't go on and on and get lost; sometimes come back home. Sometimes forget the world—those are the moments for meditation. Each day, if you want to become balanced, you

> Each day, if you want to become balanced, you should balance the outer and the inner. They should carry the same weight, so that inside you never become lopsided. This is the meaning when Zen masters say, "Walk in the river, but don't allow the water to touch your feet."

should balance the outer and the inner. They should carry the same weight, so that inside you never become lopsided.

This is the meaning when Zen masters say, "Walk in the river, but don't allow the water to touch your feet." Be in the world, but don't be of the world. Be in the world, but don't allow the world to be in you. When you come home, you come home—as if the whole world has disappeared.

Hotei, a Zen master, was passing through a village He was one of the most beautiful persons who have ever walked on earth. He was known to people as the Laughing Buddha— he used to laugh all the time. But sometimes he would sit under a tree—in this village he was sitting under a tree with closed eyes—not laughing, not even smiling, completely calm and collected. Somebody asked, "You are not laughing, Hotei?"

He opened his eyes and said, "I am preparing."

The questioner could not understand. "What do you mean by 'preparing'?"

Hotei said, "I have to prepare myself for laughter. I have to give myself a rest. I have to go in, I have to forget the whole world so that I can come back rejuvenated and I can again laugh."

If you really want to laugh, you will have to learn how to weep. If you cannot weep and if you are not capable of tears, you will become incapable of laughter. A man of laughter is also a man of tears—then a man is balanced. A man of bliss is also a man of silence. A man who is ecstatic is also a man who is centered. They both go together. And out of this togetherness of polarities a balanced being is born. And that is what the goal is.

About the Author

⤙⤙

O sho is a contemporary mystic whose life and teachings have influenced millions of people of all ages and from all walks of life. He has been described by the *Sunday Times* in London as one of the "1,000 Makers of the 20th Century" and by the *Sunday Mid-Day* (India) as one of the ten people—along with Gandhi, Nehru, and Buddha—who have changed the destiny of India.

About his own work Osho has said that he is helping to create the conditions for the birth of a new kind of human being. He has often characterized this new human being as "Zorba the Buddha"— capable of enjoying both the earthy pleasures of a Zorba the Greek and the silent serenity of a Gautama the Buddha. Running like a thread through all aspects of Osho's work is a vision that encompasses both the timeless wisdom of the East and the highest potential of Western science and technology.

He is also known for his revolutionary contribution to the science of inner transformation, with an approach to meditation that acknowledges the accelerated pace of contemporary life. His unique "Active Meditations" are designed to first release the accumulated stresses of body and mind, so that it is easier to experience the thought-free and relaxed state of meditation.

Meditation Resort

Osho Commune International

Osho Commune International, the meditation resort that Osho established in India as an oasis where his teachings could be put into practice, continues to attract thousands of visitors per year from more than one hundred different countries around the world. Located about one hundred miles southeast of Bombay in Pune, India, the facilities cover thirty-two acres in a tree-lined suburb known as Koregaon Park. The resort provides limited accommodation for guests, but there is a plentiful variety of nearby hotels.

The resort meditation programs are based on Osho's vision of a qualitatively new kind of human being who is able both to participate joyously in everyday life and to relax into silence. Most programs take place in modern, air-conditioned facilities and include everything from short to extended meditation courses, creative arts, holistic health treatments, personal growth, and the "Zen" approach to sports and recreation. Programs are offered throughout the year, alongside a full daily schedule of Osho's active meditations.

Outdoor cafes and restaurants within the resort grounds serve both traditional Indian fare and a variety of international dishes, all made with organically grown vegetables from the commune's own farm. The campus has its own private supply of safe, filtered water.

For more information: www.osho.com

This is a comprehensive Web site in different languages, featuring an on-line tour of the meditation resort, travel information, information about books and tapes, Osho information centers worldwide, and selections from Osho's talks.

Osho International
New York
e-mail: oshointernational@oshointernational.com
web: www.osho.com/oshointernational